Coney Detroit

CONEY Detroit

KATHERINE YUNG *and* JOE GRIMM

A Painted Turtle book
Detroit, Michigan

Library of Congress Cataloging-in-Publication Data

Yung, Katherine.
  Coney Detroit / Katherine Yung and Joe Grimm.
    p. cm. — (A painted turtle book)
  Includes index.
  ISBN 978-0-8143-3518-5 (pbk. : alk. paper) — ISBN 978-0-8143-3718-9 (ebook)
  1. Cooking (Frankfurters)—Michigan—Detroit. 2. Cooking, American—Midwestern style. I. Grimm, Joe. II. Title.
  TX749.Y86 2012
  641.59774'34—dc23
                        2011035812

Publication of this book was made possible through the generosity of the Ford R. Bryan Publication Fund.

Grateful acknowledgment is made to the Leonard and Harriette Simons Endowed Family Fund for the generous support of the publication of this volume.

No coneys were harmed during the making of this book...though at least 500 were ravenously consumed.

Designed and typeset by Brad Norr Design
Composed in Officina Serif, Engravers Gothic, and OPTI Jackson

With appreciation to the generations of men and women
who have worked tirelessly to keep us in coneys.

Katherine Yung would like to dedicate this book
to her husband, Rick Fischer, who introduced her
to coney island hot dogs.

Coney Detroit's writers and photographers
are donating their revenue from this book
to the Gleaners Community Food Bank.

Contents

Preface

Detroit is the heart of the Coney Nation, as you are about to see.

Nowhere else in the world will you find as many coney island restaurants, as many ways to eat coneys, or as many people who love them.

Every politician campaigning in Detroit must get photographed with a coney in hand. Athletes and music stars going for after-game or concert coneys run into fans doing the same thing.

When national media declare a coney showdown, we flock to the restaurants to cheer on our favorites like we cheer on our sports teams.

There are probably more coney island restaurants packed into the Detroit area than into the whole rest of the country. It's hard to know for certain, as there are coney island restaurants opening, closing, or moving every day.

It's not that they are unstable. Some coney islands have been serving the same food to parents, kids, and grandkids for generations. It's just because there are so dang many of them. Live here all your life and you will still hear about another great coney island from the friend you've just met. They are inescapable. But who's trying to escape them?

Detroiters are used to saying, "Let's meet at a coney," and we are reasonably certain there will be one within a mile or two of wherever we want to meet.

Michigan, home to Detroit, is a coney-loving state. You're about to learn about some great coney traditions in Flint, Jackson, Kalamazoo, Port Huron, and Traverse City. These are not offshoots of Detroit but places with coney histories all their own.

Michigan exports coneys to sentimental ex-patriots, and some of us have moved out of state and set up whole restaurants for our kind of coney islands in Nevada, Arizona, and California. In parts of New York State and Vermont, people sell a hot dog in a steamed bun with a meat sauce and chopped onions and they call it a "Michigan." We did not find anyone in Michigan selling a Michigan dog.

To be sure, coney islands have sprung up independently of Detroit. There are great ones in Massachusetts and Florida and Texas. But nowhere have coney islands caught fire like they have in Michigan.

In as much time as it takes to get served, here's how it happened: Coney island lunch counters were supercharged in downtown Detroit in the 1920s. At that time, there were so many workers packed into the city that some of them had to rent rooms for just eight hours a day—other workers rented the other hours. They had to grab lunch in a crowded hurry. Coney islands, with your food and change in front of you in just a minute or so, were the answer. Detroit supported several.

In the 1950s, Detroit's population reached a tipping point and began its descent. That decline was driven, in part, by the city having the nation's first freeways and suburban shopping centers. Enterprising coney island owners followed the crowds out to the malls and started a coney renaissance. Just as the coney craze might have peaked, it got a boost. Now they are everywhere you go.

Detroiters are a proud people, but we are not boastful. We do not claim to have invented the coney island hot dog. Despite friendly challenges between restaurants and the debate between Detroit-style and Flint-style coneys, we don't claim ours are the world's greatest—although they probably are. That is not the way of humble people.

We have simply embraced coneys, unconditionally, like no other place on Earth and we have built coney island restaurants on seemingly every corner.

For the twenty or so of us who have worked on this book, it has been a labor of love. That is, if obsession is really love. It took just two words to persuade people to pitch in: "Coney Detroit." Everyone who knows Detroit and coneys just gets it.

When I told Wayne State University Press that I had an idea for a book, they asked what it was. I said, "Coney Detroit." That was my entire pitch. Director Jane Hoehner and Editor-in-Chief Kathryn Wildfong said they wanted this book. Not one word had been written; not one photograph had been taken.

When I told Detroit Free Press reporter Katherine Yung about plans for the book—at a coney island, of course—she practically leaped from her seat and said she had to write it. She attacked the story with the thoroughness and precision of a business reporter, and she kept the heat up because she knew that some of the principals in this story were getting old. We had missed a couple and she didn't want to miss any more. She wanted them all to hold copies of this book in their hands. We lost a couple more as we worked. Anthony Keros and James Giftos passed away before the project was done, but their stories are in here.

I went through several attempts with different photographers and, although all were willing, Coney Detroit was just too big for one person. I decided we needed a group.

Enter Bobby Alcott and Ted Fines, principals in EXPOSURE. Detroit. That is a group of almost two thousand people from around metro Detroit who share a love and talent for photography. They meet up, help each other, and share ideas, and they have created a community that meets in person and online.

When I mentioned those two little words to Bobby and Ted, they were all in. They brought EXPOSURE.Detroit with them. You'll see work by ten of those photographers in this book. Often they paired up to cover assignments together. Any excuse to visit a coney island.

Wayne State University Press Assistant Editorial Manager Carrie Downes Teefey and freelance designer Brad Norr took all this work and turned it into this book.

Turn the pages and learn the Coney Detroit story. Just be sure not to drool on them.

Joe Grimm

Introduction

Michigan is the coney capital of the world.

Whether prepared Detroit-style with a beanless chili sauce or a meat topping like they do in Flint and Jackson, coney dogs have ingrained themselves in the state's culinary landscape for nearly a century.

Michigan's hundreds of coney island restaurants serve thousands of coney dogs each day. These hot dog delights have become such a key part of the state's culture that they are served at graduation parties, wedding receptions, city festivals, charitable benefits, Fourth of July picnics, and other occasions.

Nowhere in the world is as crazy about coney dogs as metro Detroit. Its beanless chili dogs are sold everywhere, from stand-alone locations to strip malls and shopping centers, from downtowns to outlying suburbs, from gas stations to Detroit Metro Airport and Comerica Park.

So many coney dogs are consumed that metro Detroit alone boasts three large chains of coney island restaurants.

The mania doesn't stop there. Children in the area sell kits containing frozen coney dogs for school fund-raisers. In downtown Detroit, one company offers walking tours of coney islands. And some local supermarkets even stock a popular brand of the beanless chili that goes on top of the hot dogs.

But what looks simple—a hot dog in a bun with onions, mustard, and either chili or a meat topping—is anything but.

For starters, the bun must be steamed. The onions should be chopped by hand. And not just any hot dog will do. Coney aficionados live for the snap of a grilled natural casing wiener.

"There are a lot of things that have to come together at the right time," says Terry Keros, one of the owners of the Kerby's Koney Island chain. "You know it's good when you want to order a second one."

What separates the best coneys from all the others is the chili or meat topping.

In Detroit, many coney islands buy a thick beanless chili made by National Chili Company and add their own blend of spices to it. Likewise, in Flint nearly all the coney islands get their meat topping from Abbott's Meat, but they mix in different spices to create their own unique flavors.

Some coney islands prefer to make their own chili or meat topping. Their homemade recipes have been passed down from one generation to the next, becoming fiercely guarded secrets.

At Jackson Coney Island in downtown Jackson, owner Lisa Creech is the only one who makes the restaurant's popular meat topping. She says people have offered her employees money for the recipe.

"It's very hard to season," Creech admits. "If you put too much of something, you can really taste it."

Knowing what makes a good coney dog is the easy part. Learning how to eat them like a pro requires skill honed from years of practice.

The most avid coney dog fans can quickly devour these treats without the aid of a fork or knife and without getting any mustard, onions, chili, or meat topping on their shirt or pants.

This sounds easy—to anyone who has never eaten a coney dog.

While mastering the art of eating a coney is all about fun, there's more to these hot dogs than what you see on the plate.

For decades, coney islands have provided a livelihood for immigrants from Greece and Macedonia who arrived in the United States with only a few dollars, speaking little or no English and lacking any formal education. For many of these newcomers, coney islands became their ticket to the American dream after years of hard work.

Today many of these first-generation immigrants have retired and their children and grandchildren are running the restaurants. But the Greeks and Macedonians no longer have the business to themselves. Albanians now operate many coney islands in metro Detroit as they, too, have discovered the appeal of coney dogs.

"It's something easy you can start with," explains John Qafa, owner of one of the L. George's Coney Islands, the largest Albanian-owned coney chain. "If you want to work and if you want to dedicate your time, you can become successful."

It's difficult to say for sure who started the first coney island. Despite many claims by different restaurants, it appears that several Greek immigrants all started selling coney dogs in the early part of the twentieth century, not just in Michigan but also in Massachusetts, Florida, Texas, and other states.

The Greeks didn't bring hot dogs from their native land. But many of them passed through New York's Ellis Island and heard about or visited Coney Island, later borrowing this name for their hot dogs, according to one legend. Why they took a fancy to this food remains a mystery.

Though these immigrants started successful coney islands in several states, only in Michigan did these restaurants really take off, evolving over time into a booming industry with hundreds of locations.

Value for the money has always been a key part of coney dogs' appeal, especially in a state that has weathered its share of ups and downs. But traditions also play a role.

"It's just like Philly cheese steaks or Chicago deep dish pizza," says Tom Giftos Jr., who runs the National Coney Island chain. "People grow up with it."

Much of the growth of Detroit's coney islands can be traced to the Keros family. When brothers William "Bill" and Constantine "Gust" Keros opened Lafayette and American Coney Islands in downtown Detroit in the 1920s and 1930s, they probably never imagined they were planting the seeds for a bumper crop of coney islands to come.

"We wouldn't be here without them," says Mark Mitchell, co-owner of Athens Coney Island in Royal Oak.

Some of the Keros brothers' family members and many of their employees went on to open their own successful coney islands, taking the concept into Detroit's suburbs. They found plenty of hungry customers at shopping malls, which the region helped pioneer.

The situation proved similar in Flint. Many of the city's first coney islands were started by employees who worked at Flint's Original Coney Island, which created the Flint-style coney dog.

Coney islands have come a long way since those early days. Most of these family businesses now offer elaborate menus featuring Greek salads, omelettes, and steaks, going far beyond coney dogs.

In some ways, these coney islands are Michigan's version of the diners popular in other states, like New Jersey. Some coney islands, such as Athens and the National Coney Islands, were even built to look like diners.

Only a small number of coney islands still focus solely on coney dogs. They are some of the oldest ones, located mostly in the downtowns of cities. These coney islands grill their hot dogs near their front windows. When they opened for business, hot dogs came in links and buns were sliced by hand.

At these coney islands, no menus are required. These restaurants refuse to change with the times, keeping the same worn counters, stools, and booths from yesteryear. Many don't even accept credit cards.

Walking into one of these places is like going back to a simpler time, though a coney can no longer be had for a nickel.

"I would bend over backwards before I ever change anything," says Todd Irish, owner of Walt's Original Coney Island, which started in downtown Pontiac in 1936 and is now located in Waterford. "We live and die by the coney."

But all coney islands, whether old or new, share one thing in common. They attract all kinds of people, from celebrities, politicians, and millionaires to those barely scraping by.

"We have a guy who doesn't have two nickels to rub together and one of the richest men in town," Bill Pozios says of the customers who frequent his Mama Vicki's Coney Island in Port Huron.

This type of popularity helps explain why the coney dog is Michigan's signature food. After all, the state is the undisputed coney king.

Just ask coney island owners. They love to tell stories about customers who move to other states. When these ex-residents come back for a visit, they usually head straight from the airport to a coney island.

"I have a lot of people like that," says Leo Stassinopoulos, co-owner of the Leo's Coney Island chain. "They say, 'I can't go home first. I've got to have a hot dog and a salad before I go home.'"

IT IS NO PROBLEM FOR A THIRTY-YEAR CONEYMAN LIKE JERRY ABU EL HAWA TO DELIVER FOUR, FIVE, SIX, OR MORE PLATES OF CONEYS AND FRIES—AND TO STILL HAVE ONE HAND FREE FOR TALKING.

Photo by Keith Burgess

Lafayette and American Coney Islands

Though Michigan has many unique and beloved coney islands, none are as legendary as the Lafayette and American Coney Islands at the crossroads of Michigan Avenue and West Lafayette Boulevard in downtown Detroit.

Metro Detroiters can thank these two side-by-side coney islands for sparking the region's love affair with coney dogs. Many of the operators of today's popular coney islands got their training at Lafayette or American or are related to their founders, brothers William "Bill" and Constantine "Gust" Keros.

Despite their shared history, the two coney islands are constantly engaged in a never-ending battle—some describe it as a feud—over who has the best coney dogs.

Lafayette has won the hearts of many longtime Detroit residents by keeping everything almost the same as when Bill Keros began selling coney dogs in the early 1920s. Stepping into Lafayette is like going back in time, with its old-fashioned counters, short stools, and tiled walls.

American, on the other hand, looks brighter and newer. With its red chairs and white tables, it plays up its patriotic name. It has tried to change with the times but still preserve its rich heritage.

Both coney islands started out as tiny restaurants. But in 1968, Lafayette doubled its size by taking over the space behind it, gaining an entrance on Michigan Avenue. Similarly, in 1991 American knocked down a wall and expanded east into the former United Shirt building.

Over the years, both have added French fries to their menus and switched from soda bottles to fountain drinks and cans. Both buy their hot dogs from Dearborn Sausage and their buns from Metropolitan Baking Company in Hamtramck. And both use a salad-style yellow mustard to make their mouthwatering coneys.

But that's where the similarities end.

Though coney dogs remain king at both restaurants, American has introduced other kinds of foods, like gyro sandwiches and fried fish. Not so at Lafayette, where the small black menu board on one wall was last changed more than ten years ago.

Other differences are more subtle. American accepts credit and debit cards

That's how we do it. The no-hesitation, bare-handed, straight-ahead way to hold and eat a coney. This one is going down easy at American Coney Island, where the forks delivered with the coneys are, for some people, merely decorative. *(Photo by Keith Burgess)*

while Lafayette takes only cash. American serves Pepsi while Lafayette customers drink Coke. And Sweet Vidalia onions top American's coneys while Lafayette uses Spanish ones.

But nothing is more important than the chili.

American's tastes a bit spicier while Lafayette's is beefier. Lafayette uses a secret Keros family recipe mixed in with a little chili from National Chili Company. American makes its own chili at a company it partly owns called Detroit Chili Company.

"The chili is the main thing," says Ali Alhalmi, one of Lafayette's owners who usually can be seen tending the grill near the restaurant's front window.

He proudly notes that his coney island goes through at least three hundred pounds of ground hamburger a week.

At both restaurants, the chili recipes are closely guarded. "It's basically meat, spices, and onions," says Danny Keros, American's general manager and Gust's grandson. "There are a few other things, but I can't give you the whole secret."

Things weren't always this way. According to Danny, both coney islands started out using the same hot dogs and the same chili. "Everything was exactly the same," he says. "There was no difference."

Today the intense rivalry between Lafayette and American even includes a debate over which coney island opened first. American's current operators, Danny and his cousin Grace Keros, like to boast that their restaurant dates back to 1917. Meanwhile, the owners of Lafayette claim the coney island got its start in 1914.

American Coney Island expanded out to the point of its flat-iron shaped building where West Lafayette Boulevard and Michigan Avenue pinch together near Detroit's Campus Martius. The table at the tip is great for people watching—or being watched. It can be hot on sunny mornings. (Photo by Rob Terwilliger)

Detroit city directories from the early twentieth century portray things differently.

Other coney islands existed in Detroit before American and Lafayette. Records show the names of two other coney islands on West Lafayette Boulevard—the Original Coney Island and Orpheum Coney Island—though they didn't last long.

According to the directories, Lafayette Coney Island opened in 1923. Gust and Bill operated the coney island at 114 West Lafayette Boulevard, where American stands today.

In the mid-1920s, the restaurant changed its name to the Lafayette Lunch Company. But differences between the brothers

Newcomers are surprised to see two coney island restaurants right next door to each other. Veterans take it for granted. There once was a third right next to Lafayette: State Coney Island. *(Photo by Keith Burgess)*

caused them to split up. The directories show that in 1931, Bill opened his own restaurant next door at 118 West Lafayette Boulevard, Lafayette's current and only home, while Gust ran a hat-cleaning business.

But in 1936 Gust launched his own restaurant, which became the American Coney Island. A year later, Bill went back to using the Lafayette Coney Island name.

Gust and Bill were sheep herders from Dara, a small village in

Lafayette Coney Island's interior has remained plain and largely unchanged for decades. That, for some, is part of the appeal. *(Photo by Ted Fines)*

southern Greece. In search of a better life, Gust moved to Detroit, where he sold popcorn from a horse-drawn wagon and shined shoes before going into the coney business.

Gust's youngest son, Chuck Keros, says that his father, who died in 1971, never put on an apron. A stylish man, Gust wore spats, Borsalino hats, and suits from Scholnick's, a Detroit haberdashery. Gust was active in local Greek organizations, helping other immigrants by hiring them for jobs at his restaurant.

"My dad was a big sport," Chuck recalls fondly. "He was very outgoing and everybody liked him.

While Gust sported a mustache, his brother, Bill, was clean shaven. Bill helped found a Greek orthodox church in Detroit but

Chuck Keros with his daughter Grace and nephew Danny in the place that best locates where it all began. *(Photo by Bobby Alcott)*

most of his life was dedicated to running Lafayette, according to his oldest son, Tony Keros. He recalls his father, who died in 1970, as a very ethical and reserved man who would work at his restaurant during the day, go home for dinner, and return to his coney island in the evenings. Bill did everything, including chopping the onions and cooking the hamburger meat.

"The Lafayette was his life," Tony says. "He ran the show."

If operating two coney islands next to each other on the same block sounds bizarre, that never bothered the Keros family. In fact, during the 1950s and 1960s, the family ran three coney islands in a row—American, Lafayette, and State Coney Island. However, they soon realized that even in Detroit there were limits to how many coney dogs you could sell on one block.

The rivalry between American and Lafayette has always been intense but burst out into the open in 1969 in what became known as the "Chili War."

Though no ground beef was thrown, before it was all over Lafayette's chili supplier, National Chili, had sued American's chili supplier for $100,000 for allegedly stealing its secret recipe. The dispute was settled before it went to court.

ALI ALHALMI, ONE OF LAFAYETTE'S OWNERS, DEFTLY FORKS UP A HOT DOG FOR A WAITING STEAMED BUN. IN SECONDS, IT WILL BE SAUCED, MUSTARDED, ONIONED, AND ON ITS WAY TO A CUSTOMER.

Photo by Keith Burgess

Today, decades later, the competition between the coney islands is just as fierce even though Lafayette is no longer owned by Bill's offspring. His son George Keros, who ran Lafayette for many years, sold the restaurant in 1993 to six of its longtime employees when he retired from the business.

One of them, Barry "Opi" Openbrier, died in 2008. But the other five, all immigrants from Yemen and Albania, work hard every day to make sure that everyone can enjoy Lafayette's coney dogs.

Loyal employees, after all, are one of the key things that distinguish Lafayette and American from many other coney islands. Some have been working at the downtown landmarks for more than three decades.

"They are always here," says Grace Keros, American's current owner and Chuck's daughter. "They care about it."

They aren't the only ones with deep ties to these coney islands.

At American, Grace regularly receives letters, phone calls, and emails from people who order her restaurant's coney kits, which are designed to give ex-Detroiters living far from home a taste of coney heaven.

These customers have told her stories about how American was where they received marriage proposals, had their first dates, and broke up with their boyfriends.

"My dad and my grandpa don't know what they've done here," Grace says. "It's the history. It's the whole nostalgia. It's the atmosphere. It's amazing."

The junction of West Lafayette Boulevard and Michigan Avenue is, for many, ground zero for all things coney. This is where the TV crews come when national food shows want to wage a coney challenge and the spawning grounds for scores of coney island restaurants. *(Photo by Keith Burgess)*

Ahmed Noman, a thirty-three-year employee at Lafayette, transfers a pot full of beef browned for loose burgers. Adding this beef on top of the chili sauce turns a coney dog into a special. *(Photo by Keith Burgess)*

A renovation brought American Coney Island a snappy, up-to-date look with a checkerboard-pattern floor and red accents. The tip of the restaurant points east, toward Detroit's Campus Martius park.

Photo by Rob Terwilliger

DULY'S PLACE IN SOUTHWEST DETROIT STILL LOOKS MUCH THE SAME AS IT DID IN THIS UNDATED PHOTO. FOUNDER DULY SEIT STANDS BEHIND THE COUNTER, MAKING SURE HIS CUSTOMERS HAVE PLENTY OF CONEY DOGS TO EAT.

Photo by Marion Toptani

Duly's Place

IT'S OUTLASTED THE STREETCARS AND AUTO FACTORIES
AND SEEN DIFFERENT IMMIGRANT GROUPS COME AND GO.
BUT EVEN AS DULY'S PLACE NEARS ITS ONE HUNDREDTH BIRTHDAY,
SOUTHWEST DETROIT'S CONEY LANDMARK HAS BARELY CHANGED.

Its customers still sit on small red stools at a long counter, with a dark brown and tin wall behind them and a tin block ceiling overhead. Duly's is still open twenty-four hours, seven days a week, at the corner of West Vernor Highway and Junction Street. And the narrow restaurant still seems to be a favorite neighborhood gathering spot, just like it was when Duly Seit first started serving his coney dogs in 1921.

"People feel like it is home," said Gjoka "Joe" Gojcaj, a longtime Duly's employee who bought the restaurant in 2000 from Seit's family.

Though Seit died in 1963, his legacy lives on at his coney island. "I saw him feed a lot of hungry people," said Frank Verriorra, who has been a regular at Duly's since he was a young child in the 1930s. "He was a man among men."

Marion Toptani, Seit's only daughter, recalls her father as a gentle, honorable, and giving man who always wore a tie and a clean white shirt to work. He fled war-torn Albania for a new life in Detroit, learning the coney business at a downtown coney island before teaming up with a partner to open his own restaurant.

Though Duly's survived the Great Depression, it didn't escape the tough times without incurring a lot of debt. Seit and his partner split and gradually business improved.

Like most coney islands, Duly's has always been a family business. Seit got plenty of help from his youngest son, Yli, and his son-in-law, Dini Toptani. They ran the restaurant after Duly Seit's death.

In 1979, Dini Toptani died. Yli Seit, whose name means "star" in Albanian, continued to operate Duly's, serving its loyal customers for nearly twenty years.

After Yli's death in early 1998, Marion Toptani took control of the coney island. To preserve her father's restaurant for future generations, she sold it to Gojcaj, an Albanian immigrant in his mid-forties who has worked at Duly's for more than twenty-five years.

Today you can find Gojcaj, his sister, and two of his older children behind Duly's counter or in its kitchen. He's added a few menu items but kept everything else the same, paying his respects to the man who introduced coney dogs to generations of southwest Detroiters.

Coney Hot Dogs

MICHIGAN HAS A KEY ADVANTAGE OVER MANY OTHER STATES
WHEN IT COMES TO MAKING CONEY DOGS. IT'S THE HOME OF
SEVERAL COMPANIES THAT SPECIALIZE IN HIGH-QUALITY
HOT DOGS.

Their beef and pork hot dogs are not filled with potato starches, mechanically separated turkey, and corn syrup. But what really sets them apart is their natural casing skin, which gives coney dogs that snap when you bite into one.

In Detroit and Flint, two hot dog producers dominate the coney island market—Koegel Meats and Dearborn Sausage. Both of these private, family-owned businesses have prospered for decades by constantly paying attention to the quality of their hot dogs, which are made from their own recipes.

Both use natural hardwood smoke to make their hot dogs, but Koegel's dogs taste slightly sweeter than Dearborn's.

Over the years, each brand has developed a loyal following. Some coney islands even display the Koegel name in their front windows.

"Hot dogs were the original fast food," says John Koegel, president of Koegel Meats.

Koegel is the grandson of Albert Koegel, a master sausage maker from Germany who opened a small retail meat market in downtown Flint in 1916. He played a key role in the creation of the Flint-style coney dog by developing a hot dog that wouldn't turn black after sitting on a flat grill for a while.

He accomplished this by removing most of the nonfat dry milk and sugar from his Vienna frank, according to John Koegel.

For most of the twentieth century, Koegel competed fiercely against its archrival, Salay Meats, also of Flint.

But Salay closed in 2003. Since then, Koegel has been the top dog in Flint, supplying all of the coney islands in Genesee County. It's also expanding south into Detroit, where it supplies hot dogs for all of the Leo's Coney Islands, among others.

There it competes with Dearborn Sausage, which makes hot dogs at its Dearborn factory for about fifty coney islands in metro Detroit, including American Coney Island, Lafayette Coney Island, and the Senate Coney Islands. Victor Kosch, a butcher from Hungary, started the company in 1946.

In coney-crazy Detroit, there's more than enough room for two leading suppliers. "We both make quality products," says Michael Kosch, vice president of Dearborn Sausage and the grandson of the company's founder.

Dearborn Sausage's Michael Kosch (*right*) with brother-in-law Todd Meier. Both are vice presidents of the company Kosch's grandfather Victor founded in 1946. It has grown to 85,000 square feet for retail and processing. (*Photo by Rob Terwilliger*)

MICHIGAN USED TO HAVE STRICTER HOT DOG QUALITY REQUIREMENTS THAN MOST OTHER STATES, WHICH MAY BE WHY ITS CONEY DOGS TASTE SO GOOD.

Photo by Rob Terwilliger

You can see why Koegel says, "Serve the curve." It is not unusual for Flint-area coneys to advertise in the windows and on the tables that they serve the local dog. *(Photo by Rob Terwilliger)*

Koegel spans the generations. John Koegel is on the right. Family members (*from left*) are his brother-in-law, Jeffry Rocco; sister, Kathryn Koegel; father, Al Koegel; and daughter, Chloe. *(Photo by Rob Terwilliger)*

Generations of Flint residents have worked to cook Koegel's hot dogs. The company began selling fine meats in 1916. *(Photo by Rob Terwilliger)*

Overhead tracks help workers hurry hot dogs through the cooking process at Koegel Meats. (*Photo by Rob Terwilliger*)

A real coney snaps back at you when you bite it because it is cooked in a natural casing that is left on. *(Photo by Rob Terwilliger)*

ARCHITECTURALLY,
NATIONAL CONEY ISLANDS CAN LOOK LIKE CLASSIC
DINERS AND RUN WITH LOTS OF NEON AND
EMBELLISHMENTS—INSIDE AND OUT.

Photo by Spike

Detroit's Coney Chains

DETROIT IS THE ONLY CITY IN THE WORLD THAT'S HOME TO
THREE MAJOR CONEY ISLAND RESTAURANT CHAINS.
THAT'S RIGHT—THREE. THAT'S IMPRESSIVE CONSIDERING
MOST CITIES DON'T EVEN HAVE ONE.

In Detroit's suburbs, Leo's Coney Island, Kerby's Koney Island, and National Coney Island are everywhere—in stand-alone locations, tucked inside malls and strip centers, and at the airport and Comerica Park.

The chains were started by Greek immigrants in the 1960s and early 1970s. One coney island led to another and another and another. Leo's has the most locations because it franchises, but most of its restaurants are on the city's west side. Kerby's also leans more toward the west, while National dominates the east side.

These chains were not the first in metro Detroit. But their predecessors, most notably Onassis Coney Island, closed many years ago.

Over the decades, Leo's, Kerby's, and National have evolved into Detroit-style diners, distinctive because of their coney dogs and a few Greek foods.

"In every area, every city, people need a diner where they can go for quick food that's inexpensive and fresh," says Terry Keros, one of six Keros family members who own Kerby's. "Coney islands have filled that niche here."

While many older coney islands focus solely on their coney dogs, the chains have expanded their menus to include all kinds of sandwiches, burgers, salads, desserts, and other items. In fact, Greek salads outsell coney dogs at Leo's.

Nevertheless, the chains take pride in their coney dogs. Leo's mixes chili from the National Chili Company with the spicier

A family operation: Van, Alex, George, Terry, and Tim Keros. When he was made to hold a Kerby's coney that close without taking a bite, Van remarked, "This is hard to do!" *(Photo by Brett J. Lawrence)*

Leo Stassinopoulos (*right*) with his brother, Pete, who gave up naming rights because he said "Leo's Coney Island" has a better ring. Customers can take home a little Leo's in the salad dressing that is usually for sale near the cash registers. *(Photo by Bobby Alcott)*

Leo's signature sauce comes from a mix of sauces. We are not at liberty to give the precise proportions. *(Photo by Bobby Alcott)*

Leo Stassinopoulos, a Keros cousin, said that when he first started working at the family's coney islands, he was surprised, not in a good way, by the mustard on the coneys. They did not have that in Greece. *(Photo by Bobby Alcott)*

Milton brand. Kerby's makes its own chili (at the Detroit Chili Company) as does National. They all use different hot dogs.

Overall, the differences between the chains are subtle, with one exception. National has a fancier, more upscale look at most of its restaurants.

Today the chains are still finding new locations to open in metro Detroit. But they are also moving outside the region. Leo's has even gone north into Flint.

Beanless chili sauce, cheese, mustard, and chopped onions can turn a hot dog or fries into heaven on a plate. *(Photo by Brett J. Lawrence)*

The late James Giftos (*left*) and Tom Giftos Jr. built a coney island empire of more than twenty restaurants—in some cases with three in a single town. *(Photo by Eric Peoples)*

Leo's Coney Island

YES, THERE REALLY IS A GUY CALLED LEO. BUT THE
METRO DETROIT CONEY ISLAND CHAIN THAT BEARS HIS NAME
COULD JUST AS EASILY HAVE BEEN CALLED "PETE'S" AFTER
HIS OLDER BROTHER AND CONEY COLLABORATOR.

Pete said, 'Leo's sounds better than Pete's Coney Island,'" Leo Stassinopoulos says. "Nobody knew the company was going to be like this."

Pete doesn't seem to mind. The Greek brothers own southeast Michigan's largest coney island chain, Leo's Coney Island. It has been rapidly expanding by selling franchises to some of the company's longtime employees and others interested in the coney business.

The brothers launched their first coney island in 1972, calling it Southfield Coney because of its location at Southfield and 12½ Mile roads. Two more coney islands would follow, but it wasn't until 1988 that the first Leo's opened in Troy.

Over the following years, Leo and Pete steadily grew their company and by 2005 had reached a point where franchising made sense.

The brothers learned the coney business from their cousins in the Keros family. Leo worked part-time at the first Kerby's Koney Island at the Tel-Twelve Mall in Southfield, owned by Gus Keros and his brothers. They are the nephews of William and Gust Keros, the founders of the Lafayette and American Coney Islands in downtown Detroit.

Pete got his training at a coney island in the Northland Center in Southfield that was owned by his cousin Chuck Keros, Gust's son who ran the American Coney Island for many years.

It was Chuck Keros who first showed Leo that coney dogs could be the ticket to the American dream. When Leo was a teenager in the mid-1960s, Chuck came to visit his Greek village, arriving in a black limousine that was too big for the country's small roads.

Impressed, Leo asked his cousin what he did in America. But when Chuck told him he was in the coney island business, Leo didn't know what that was.

Leo has come a long way since those days, but he and Pete still keep their focus on the key ingredients for coney island success—good food and fast service.

"When a customer walks in, he has to have water a minute later and the waitress should be at the table," Leo says. "People want to get in and out quickly."

Pete and Leo take a break after a midday rush at their coney island in Farmington Hills. *(Photo by Bobby Alcott)*

National Coney Island

NATIONAL CONEY ISLAND IS THE OLDEST AND THE MOST INNOVATIVE OF DETROIT'S CONEY ISLAND CHAINS. FOUNDER JAMES GIFTOS STARTED OUT WITH A CHILI BUSINESS, NATIONAL CHILI COMPANY, BUT COULDN'T RESIST OPENING HIS OWN RESTAURANTS.

In 1965, the Greek immigrant launched his first coney island at the Macomb Mall in Roseville, Michigan. Today National Coney Island operates more than twenty-three restaurants, including three at Detroit Metro Airport.

At last count, National was racking up $25 million in sales and selling 1.6 million coney dogs a year.

The chain took its name from the chili company, which does business with many other coney islands in the region. Growth was slow and steady until the mid-1980s when National rapidly expanded, opening up a lot of glitzier restaurants with brass fixtures and neon lights.

Unlike its rivals, the chain aggressively markets its coney islands, advertising at Detroit sports games and selling its coney dogs at popular local events like Autorama. The chain even has its own logo, a chef with a mustache holding a coney dog. It calls him Mr. Pop, short for Papadopoulos.

In 2005 National celebrated its fortieth anniversary by making a forty-foot-long coney dog. But the company fell short of setting a record for the world's longest hot dog because the bun it used came in two pieces, not one.

In recent years, Giftos's son, Tom Giftos Jr., has been running National. The family's involvement in Detroit's restaurant industry started with his grandfather, also called Tom. He worked at the Lafayette Coney Island in downtown Detroit and then opened a small family diner in the city.

In the future, expect to see an increasing number of smaller "express" versions of National's coney islands at high-traffic venues like airports, stadiums, and college campuses. "We're trying to think outside the box," Tom Giftos Jr. says.

James Giftos, a native of Kyparrissia, Greece, became a partner in the National Chili Company of Detroit and opened the first National Coney Island in Macomb Mall in 1965. National is the Detroit area's dominant east-side chain. James Giftos died in 2011. *(Photo by Spike)*

Kerby's Koney Island

THOUGH THE KEROS FAMILY IS BEST KNOWN FOR
THE LAFAYETTE AND AMERICAN CONEY ISLANDS, THEY HAVE ALSO
PLAYED A KEY ROLE IN SATISFYING THE CRAVINGS
FOR CONEYS IN DETROIT'S SUBURBS.

One branch of the family owns Kerby's Koney Island, one of metro Detroit's three major coney chains. Four Keros brothers—Tim, Bill, Van, and the late Gus—learned the business at their uncles' famous downtown Detroit coney islands. They opened their first restaurant at the Tel-Twelve Mall in Southfield in 1968.

At first they used the name "Koney Island Inn." But they soon switched to the catchier "Kerby's," which is a play on the words "Keros brothers" with a "y's" added to the end.

Today Gus's three sons—Terry, George, and Alex—also work in the family business.

"The six of us get along pretty well," says Terry Keros, who has worked at coney islands since he was seven years old. "We may argue but five minutes later you're buddies again and you're back to work and running the stores."

At last count, Kerby's had twenty-four restaurants. The original one at the Tel-Twelve Mall was torn down. The chain's oldest coney island is at the Lakeside Mall in Sterling Heights. Kerby's newer locations are decorated with historical photos of downtown Detroit landmarks.

Coney dogs are still the top seller at this chain. But if you think serving thousands of these hot dogs sounds easy, think again. "It's a lot of hours," Terry Keros says. "You are working seven days a week. And your cell phone is always ringing."

Yet this coney fan, who earned a law degree from the University of Detroit, wouldn't trade his job for any other. "I really like dealing with people and the employees and just being out there," he says. "There's never a dull day in this business."

Hot dogs at different stages of grilling with buns at the ready. (*Photo by Brett J. Lawrence*)

Coney Buns

ONE OF THE REASONS WHY CONEY DOGS
TASTE SO GOOD IN DETROIT HAS NOTHING
TO DO WITH CHILI OR HOT DOGS.
IT'S ALL ABOUT THE BUNS.

Not just any buns will do. They must be made the old-fashioned way, using the sponge dough method for a better taste and smell. And they must be served fresh and warm.

For decades, Bluebird and Brown's Bun Baking Company supplied hot dog buns to nearly all of the coney islands in southeastern Michigan. But when Bluebird shut down more than ten years ago, Metropolitan Baking Company in Hamtramck began making hot dog buns. Today Brown's and Metropolitan dominate the local market.

Like most of the coney islands they supply, Brown's and Metropolitan are family-owned businesses. Charles Brown, whose last name in Macedonia was Branoff, opened his Detroit bakery in 1929, just down the street from Duly's coney island. In 1945, George Kordas launched his bread business in Hamtramck at the same location where the company operates today.

Kordas's son, Jim, and his grandson, also called George, now run Metropolitan. At Brown's, Michael Dinu, Brown's great-grandson, is taking the bakery into its eighth decade.

Brown's makes special "classic" buns for coney islands that hold up well in a steamer. Its customers that sell a lot of coney dogs prefer this bun over the company's softer, traditional one.

Metropolitan makes one kind of hot dog bun, which it calls the coney island steamer.

Though Brown's and Metropolitan used to deliver their buns to coney islands, they now rely on independent distributors to do this work. So in the wee hours every morning while many coney dog lovers are still sleeping, their hot dog buns are being picked up at the loading docks at Brown's and Metropolitan, the first step in the journey toward their stomachs.

Rack 'n' roll: Metropolitan Baking Company in Hamtramck kicks out thousands of hot dog and hamburger buns a day and is one of two major suppliers to coney island restaurants. The other major local supplier is Brown's Bun Baking Company in southwest Detroit. *(Photo by Ted Fines)*

George Kordas shows his pride in being one of the main suppliers of buns to coney islands throughout the Detroit area. If you want to visit a lot of coney islands, hitch a ride on a bread truck. *(Photo by Ted Fines)*

The hottest fires make the softest buns, to tweak Eminem's Chrysler commercial. An industrial conveyor-line oven and stacks and stacks of racks and pans dwarf two bakers on either side of the oven. Find them. *(Photo by Ted Fines)*

Coney Island Steamers—ahh!—that's the way one should be on a good coney—steamed. *(Photo by Ted Fines)*

The Coney Mall Pioneer

IN METRO DETROIT, TAKING A BREAK TO EAT SOME CONEY DOGS
WHILE SHOPPING AT THE MALL IS PART OF EVERYDAY LIFE.
BUT IT WASN'T ALWAYS THAT WAY.

The late Anthony "Tony" Keros, the oldest son of the founder of Lafayette Coney Island, is largely responsible for why coney islands exist at many Detroit-area malls today.

In February 1959, Keros opened his first coney island at Eastland Center in Harper Woods. It was called Eastland Coney Island. The Lafayette name wouldn't be used until a few years later.

"It took a couple of months for it to really take off," Keros recalled, noting that many people knew him because he had worked at his father's famous coney island.

Over the following years, Keros went on to launch coney islands at just about every major shopping mall in metro Detroit and beyond, including Westland, Southland, Oakland, and Briarwood. Business was so good that he ended up with a chain of sixteen restaurants, all under the Lafayette name.

By the time Keros retired in 2006, he had sold each of his coney islands. A few are now owned by some of his cousins who run the Kerby's Koney Island chain.

Athens Coney Island

NO TOUR OF METRO DETROIT'S CONEY SCENE
WOULD BE COMPLETE WITHOUT A STOP
AT ATHENS CONEY ISLAND.

This Royal Oak favorite has been attracting coney lovers since it opened its doors in September 1964. Back then, Athens could seat only a dozen customers. Its dining area consisted of five stools and a few small tables. And all it sold were coneys, loose hamburgers, and bean soup.

Athens's founder, William Lipson, left the vending machine business to sell coney dogs. Though he wasn't Greek, Lipson named his restaurant "Athens" since almost all the coney islands at that time were owned by immigrants from Greece. The name may have helped because a few years later, Lipson expanded Athens to forty seats.

In 1978, Lipson wanted to retire and sold Athens to two young Greek brothers, Mark and Greg Mitchell. They often ate at Athens because their father owned a dry-cleaning business just up Woodward Avenue.

"We were both looking for something to do," Mark Mitchell says. "Athens was successful."

Though the brothers were only in their twenties and had no previous restaurant experience, many of the coney island's employees stayed on, helping them learn the business.

One of them, Cynthia Stevens, still works at Athens. "She's the glue that holds the whole place together," Mark Mitchell says. "You can't teach what she has inside her— loyalty, honesty, wanting to do a good job."

The Mitchell brothers continue to use Lipson's recipes for chili and bean soup, but they have added salads, chicken sandwiches, and other foods to the menu. Coney dogs are still the top draw.

Though the Mitchells renovated Athens in 1988—adding new floors, new walls, and a new ceiling—the brothers always knew they would outgrow the restaurant's building. In August 2002, they moved their coney island next door into new space designed to resemble a 1950s diner with red leather booths, posters of vintage Chevrolets, and red neon lights around the ceiling. The restaurant's former location is now Athens's parking lot.

Athens Coney Island has been satisfying coney diners along one of the Detroit area's busiest streets since 1964. It has grown from a dozen seats to ninety-two. Woodward Avenue is home to the first mile of paved concrete roads in the United States and about a dozen coney island restaurants. The diner-style architecture of Athens makes it stand out. *(Photo by Rob Terwilliger)*

The expansion helped boost Athens's popularity, which reaches new heights every August during the Woodward Dream Cruise, the nation's biggest classic car event. In recent years, the coney island has served as General Motors' cruise headquarters, the place where the automaker entertains its dealers, suppliers, and customers.

"It's turned into a holiday," Mark Mitchell says of the ten-day celebration, Athens's busiest time of the year.

For all their success, the Mitchells haven't forgotten Lipson, who died a few months before Athens moved to its current location. A picture of him hangs by the coney island's front door.

Just the right touch. Matt Peterson dresses a couple dogs at Athens Coney Island. Brown's buns, like those in the bags on the shelves, are one of the standards at Detroit coneys. The other top choice is Metropolitan's coney steamers. *(Photo by Rob Terwilliger)*

Photo by Rob Terwilliger

NAPKINS—AND PLENTY OF THEM—MIGHT BE A GOOD CONEY DOG'S SIXTH INGREDIENT, RIGHT AFTER BUN, HOT DOG, CHILI SAUCE, ONIONS, AND MUSTARD.

The sign says it all. With such a heavy Greek influence on Detroit's early coney islands, many names are Greek, even if the owners are not. Besides Athens, coney names with Grecian inspiration include Athenian, Greek Islands, Hellenic, Olympic, Apollo, and Zorba's. *(Photo by Rob Terwilliger)*

Mark Mitchell gets demonstrative as he chats with counter customers at his Athens Coney Island. *(Photo by Rob Terwilliger)*

Counter Culture

THE CONEY ISLAND COUNTER IS A GREAT EQUALIZER.
WHEN YOU BELLY UP TO THE COUNTER AND PLOP DOWN
ON ONE OF THOSE STOOLS—THEY ARE USUALLY RED—
YOU ARE IN CONEY SPACE.

It matters not whether the person next to you is a millionaire or a pauper; you might sit next to either at a coney counter. But as you eat, bank account and station do not matter. You are cut from the same cloth. You are equals, enjoying your shared taste for coneys and the places that make them. Feel free to catch up with an old friend, make friends with the new one on the stool next to yours, or enjoy your meal in one of the day's quiet interludes. It's all up to you. The one thing you can't do at a coney counter is put on airs.

While most coney islands have tables—at least a few of them, big enough for two—counter seating is a hallmark of the finest traditional coney island restaurant.

The bill says 2E, which means two with everything, or "two up," at Virginia Coney Island in Jackson. *(Photo by Rob Terwilliger)*

A coney island counter is a great equalizer. White collar and blue collar, male and female, old and young sit down side by side and eat the same fare. Until they go back to their jobs and lives on the outside, they are in coney space. This is the counter at the classic Coney Island Sandwich Shop in St. Petersburg, Florida. *(Photo by Brian Blanco)*

Don't you dare reach for that catsup on the counter at Kalamazoo's Coney Island Lunch. Catsup is for the fries, and we don't see any. Putting catsup on a coney can get you tossed out of a place. Knife and fork are optional. Napkins? Mandatory. *(Photo by Rob Terwilliger)*

The checkerboard motif at American Coney Island in downtown Detroit is reflected in its stainless steel stools, a standard fixture at many coney counters. *(Photo by Rob Terwilliger)*

THERE IS COMFORT IN EATING AT A CONEY ISLAND COUNTER. YOU'RE FREE TO LOOK STRAIGHT AHEAD IN CONEY CONCENTRATION OR STRIKE UP A CONVERSATION. THIS IS VIRGINIA CONEY ISLAND IN JACKSON.

Photo by Rob Terwilliger

PETE'S UNIQUE, TWIN HORSESHOE COUNTERS MAKE FRIENDS AND STRANGERS FACE EACH OTHER OVER THEIR MEALS. THE CURVING COUNTERS ARE AN ATTRACTION.

Photo by Bobby Alcott

Pontiac's Historic Coney Islands

DOWNTOWN DETROIT WASN'T THE ONLY PLACE THAT ONCE HAD
THREE CONEY ISLANDS IN A ROW. FROM 1936 UNTIL 1964, PONTIAC,
MICHIGAN, WAS A CONEY LOVER'S DREAM.

Back then, thousands of coney fans flocked to the corner of Saginaw and Jackson streets to indulge their passion at Pete's Coney Island, Walt's Original Coney Island, and Angel's Coney Island.

Pete Traicoff, an immigrant from Macedonia, opened the oldest of the coney islands, Pete's, in the 1920s. It started out as a peanut stand, selling hot peanuts, sandwiches, and coffee before adding hot dogs. Over the next few decades, Traicoff was so successful that he tore down his restaurant twice in order to build bigger buildings.

Demand for coney dogs reached such lofty heights that in 1936, Traicoff's son, Walt, opened his own coney island next door.

After many years of success, in 1964 the trio of coney islands was forced to break up when the city of Pontiac ordered them to move to make way for a new building. Today Angel's no longer exists, but Pete's and Walt's are still serving customers at different locations.

At both restaurants, coney dogs are the main attraction. After getting the boot from Pontiac, Walt's moved to its present location on M-59 in Waterford. Many of his customers followed him, and the restaurant, which consisted of a small counter and three tables, did well.

In the mid-1970s, Walt Traicoff sold his coney island. The new owner ran it for only two and a half years before handing it over to real estate broker Todd Irish in 1978.

Irish, a longtime Walt's customer, has owned the coney island ever since, making some big changes. He added a drive-thru window and booths and removed one of the bathrooms, increasing the number of seats from fourteen to twenty-four. And he transformed Walt's plain interior into a colorful haven of American memorabilia.

Almost every inch of Walt's walls and ceiling is covered by eye-catching mementos such as antique gas station signs, a huge cut-out of a vintage Ford Thunderbird, and Irish's collection of old movie posters, many from the former Huron Theatre. Half of the decorations came from the coney island's customers.

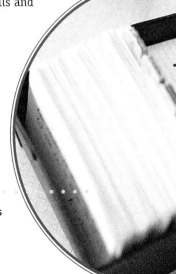

A box of customer stories and memories at Walt's. *(Photo by Ryan Southen)*

But Irish hasn't altered one key thing: Walt's coney dogs. Their taste is still the same as when Walt Traicoff made them.

"It would have been absolute suicide to change anything," says Irish, who says he has eaten more than seventeen thousand hot dogs.

"I love the flavor, the richness" of coney dogs, he adds. "They are unique."

Down the street from Walt's, two Traicoffs, Tom and his son Mike, operate Pete's Coney Island. Tom Traicoff is Pete's grandson and the third generation to run the family business.

When Pete's was forced to leave downtown Pontiac in 1964, it stayed in the city, moving to a site on Orchard Lake Road before settling at its current location in 1974.

Pete's has spawned some offspring. Tom Traicoff's brother, Ed Zull, owns Pete's Coney Island II, with locations in Clarkston and Lake Orion.

For Tom Traicoff, nothing is more important than keeping Pete's true to its heritage. The restaurant features two horseshoe-shaped counters, just like it used to have in downtown Pontiac.

"Nothing has changed," says the coney veteran, who's been in the business for more than fifty years. "Eating a hot dog is quick and easy and it's cheap. Two coneys and a glass of water are four bucks. That's why we are still in business."

Years of operation and a Macedonian heritage line the walls at Pete's Coney Island. The couple in the photo on the wall are founder and namesake, Pete Traicoff, and his wife, Donna. *(Photo by Bobby Alcott)*

This ersatz dog is a perch for Superman, Underdog, Santa Claus, the Lone
Ranger, and a dinosaur. Unusual in other locations, but just right at Walt's.
(Photo by Ryan Southen)

THE INSIDE—AND PART OF THE OUTSIDE, TOO—IS A TREAT OR AN ATTACK ON THE EYES, DEPENDING ON THE BEHOLDER. YOU CAN GIVE THE BLAME OR CREDIT TO OWNER TODD IRISH.

Photo by Ryan Southen

Pete's Coney Island had its roots in downtown Pontiac as one in a row of three adjacent coney island restaurants. It has moved but stays true to its original roots and menu. *(Photo by Bobby Alcott)*

Manager Les Finkelstein handles day-to-day operations at Walt's. *(Photo by Ryan Southen)*

Before he bought the place, Todd Irish did his work on the other side of the counter, polishing off coney dogs. Irish estimates he has eaten seventeen thousand. *(Photo by Ryan Southen)*

Flint-Style Coney Dogs

ABOUT AN HOUR'S DRIVE NORTH OF DETROIT LIES A DIFFERENT
KIND OF CONEY PARADISE WITH A RICH HISTORY. FLINT, MICHIGAN,
IS BEST KNOWN AS THE BIRTHPLACE OF GENERAL MOTORS,
BUT ITS CONEY DOGS ARE ALSO FAMOUS.

Many Detroiters on their way up north are surprised when they stop for a coney dog in Flint. These coneys are served with a loose meat topping, not the beanless chili that's the hallmark of Detroit-style coneys. But everything else is the same—the hot dog, steamed bun, mustard, and onions. Many Detroiters find these coneys dry, but for Flint residents they're heavenly.

In Flint, the meat topping is called sauce, and its taste varies slightly from coney island to coney island, depending on what kinds of spices are added. Nearly every coney island in the city buys its meat topping from Abbott's Meat and its hot dogs from Koegel Meats, both longtime Flint businesses.

As a result, the variations in taste among coney dogs in Flint are not as great as in metro Detroit, where the type of chili and hot dogs used can vary dramatically from one coney island to the next.

In Flint, the differences are more subtle, with one coney dog a tad spicier than another. It all depends on how much cumin, chili powder, and other seasonings are added.

Some coney islands even buy their sauce from Abbott's with many of the spices already mixed in.

What's the secret to a good Flint coney dog? "The sauce has to be hot and it has to be fresh," says Kosta Popoff, owner of Starlite Coney Island, which makes three or four pots of its sauce every day.

Though Abbott's meat topping looks like ground beef, it's actually ground beef and beef hearts, says Ed Abbott, who shares the same name as his grandfather, who started the meat processing business in 1907.

Abbott's Meat played a crucial role in creating the Flint-style coney dog. Simeon "Sam" Brayan, an immigrant from Macedonia, worked with the late Ed Abbott to concoct a meat topping for hot dogs that's loose and crumbles. The same recipe is still used today.

Finding the perfect hot dog also took some experimenting. Brayan turned to German sausage maker Albert Koegel, who at the time ran a small meat market in downtown Flint. Because Koegel's popular Vienna franks would turn black on the grills

Known for miles, Starlite Coney Island serves up the traditional Flint-style meat topping and is open twenty-four hours a day. Waffled aluminum walls inside and out and a tall sign with three kinds of lighting make it a beacon in the night. (*Photo by Bobby Alcott*)

used by coney islands, he decided to remove the nonfat dry milk and sugar in these hot dogs. That solved the problem.

With these hurdles behind him, Brayan and two partners, George Brown and Nick George, opened Flint's Original Coney Island on Saginaw Street in 1919. According to *Two to Go—A Short History of Flint's Coney Island Restaurants*, the Original sold four thousand coney dogs a day during its heyday from 1924 to 1926.

Ed Abbott fondly recalls the hot dogs cooking on the grill in the Original's front window. Open twenty-four hours, the coney island had two front doors with long counters inside. Brayan was a "little guy but hardworking and you could see him eyeing that counter," Abbott says.

As a Catholic, Abbott couldn't eat meat on Fridays. But when he was a teenager, his father would often ask him to run down to the Original for some coney dogs—just before midnight.

"You'd get five, six, seven in a bag and go back home and sit on the floor," Abbott remembers. "My mom would be sleeping. She'd wake me up mad because the room reeked of onions and chili."

Albert Koegel, the founder of Koegel Meats, and his son, also called Albert, used to eat lunch at the Original every Saturday. Back then, two coney dogs and a glass of milk cost twenty-five cents.

A Flint or Detroit combination: coneys and cars. Hey! Don't drip any sauce on the paint. *(Photo by Rob Terwilliger)*

Orders up! The newer coney island chains serve a lot of breakfasts, salads, hamburgers, and grilled cheese sandwiches. Coney island hot dogs can be a small part of what they do. Did we mention fries? *(Photo by Rob Terwilliger)*

BREAKFAST
& LUNCH
SPECIALS
DAILY

Angelo's
CONEY ISLAND
SERVING FLINT SINCE 1949

HAVE YOU HAD 2 LATELY
?

CHECK O
★ OUR
★ DAILY
★ SPECIAL

TRY OUR
HARD SHELL
CONEY

THE REAL
Angelo's
IS BACK!!
"THE OLD OWNER IS BACK!"

THURSDAY
GRILLED CHEESE
TOMATO SOUP
$2.50

MICHIGAN
BCL 3124

The Original proved so popular that other coney islands sprang up in the same area, forming a hub of sorts around the intersection of Saginaw and Water streets.

None of these downtown coney islands is still operating today, including the Original, which ended its long run in 1979. Since then, Angelo's Coney Island on Davison Road has been the place to chow down on Flint-style coney dogs.

Angelo's has served hungry Flint residents ever since Macedonian immigrants Carl Paul and Angelo Nikiloff opened the place in 1949. It has switched owners a few times through the years, but none has dared to tinker with its beloved coney dogs.

"This is like eating your mother's food," says Flint native Neil Helmkay, Angelo's current owner, who keeps the restaurant open twenty-four hours nearly every day of the year.

As the decades have gone by, the dividing line between Flint-style coneys and Detroit-style ones is getting a little blurry. Diners at Mega Coney Island, which has locations in Flint and Fenton, can order both types of coney dogs.

Angelo's Coney Island, a popular place for coneys in Flint, has changed hands a number of times, but its name, from co-founder Angelo Nikiloff, is a bankable constant. *(Photo by Bobby Alcott)*

The coney island hot dog has inspired a number of imitations. In addition to varieties of coney tacos, there are coney omelettes, coney pizzas, and coney wraps. *(Photo by Bobby Alcott)*

Rocky Dedivanaj, one of Mega's owners, says that the restaurant's Fenton location, south of Flint, sells just as many Detroit-style coneys as Flint ones.

If two kinds of coneys under one roof are not mindboggling enough, Mega has another surprise: the Mega Special, a coney dog with both Detroit-style chili and Flint coney sauce.

That's not the only way that lines are being crossed. The Leo's Coney Island chain in Detroit has migrated north and offers both types of coney dogs at its Flint locations. Many Flint coney islands use hot dog buns from Detroit bakeries.

And more than fifteen years ago, Koegel Meats started making chili for Detroit-style coney dogs at its plant near Flint's airport. Koegel created its own recipe for the chili, which is used by many coney islands in Detroit's suburbs.

Drive-in windows are available at Flint's top coney islands—Starlite and Angelo's—but they are the exception, rather than the rule, in other cities. Even less common, but it does happen: deliveries. *(Photo by Bobby Alcott)*

Starlite and other Flint coney islands call this meat topping a sauce, but they make it drier than Detroit places do. Detroiters and people in Flint are loyal to their local styles. Though they may sample the other kind, they seem to stick with what they've grown up on. *(Photo by Bobby Alcott)*

Mega Coney Island, with locations in and around Flint, is big because it needs to be. Mega caters to all, with side-by-side Flint- and Detroit-style coneys, if you want to run your own taste test. *(Photo by Rob Terwilliger)*

Mega is a Dedivanaj family affair. Front row, from left: Christian, Shpresa, and Adem. Back row, from left: Ilyrjana, Violet, Valbon, Marlena, Gjergj, Rrok, Tereze, Drit, and Jozef. *(Photo by Rob Terwilliger)*

JACKSON CONEY ISLAND
IS ONE OF TWO HISTORIC CONEY ISLANDS THAT OPERATE
ON THE SAME BLOCK, ABOUT SEVENTY-FIVE MILES DUE
WEST OF DETROIT.

Photo by Rob Terwilliger

Jackson Coneys

THE RESIDENTS OF JACKSON, MICHIGAN, SHOULD BE FORGIVEN
IF THEY TAKE THEIR CONEY DOGS FOR GRANTED. SINCE THE MID-1930s
THIS CITY WEST OF ANN ARBOR HAS OFFERED AN ABUNDANCE
OF THESE HOT DOG DELIGHTS.

Today Jackson is one of the few places that can boast about having two historic coney islands on the same downtown block.

Generations of Jackson residents grew up eating coney dogs at Jackson Coney Island, Virginia Coney Island, or both. If Jackson got too busy, they could head to the other side of the block to grab some coneys at Virginia and vice versa.

After all, it's difficult to tell the difference between the rivals' Flint-style coney dogs. They both use the same hot dogs from Gordon Food Service, grilled near their front windows. They both use beef hearts to make their homemade meat topping, which tastes very similar. And they both offer fried onions instead of raw ones, if that's what customers prefer.

Jackson, however, uses hot dog buns baked in Detroit while those at Virginia come from a local bakery.

The lack of differentiation hasn't hurt either restaurant, and both continue to fuel the city's coney mania.

"There's really no competition," Lisa Creech, Jackson's owner, says of Virginia. "We help each other."

Though each coney island has its own loyal fans who refuse to go to the other side of the block, the restaurants share some historical ties, along with their old-fashioned counters, stools, and menu boards.

The two men who ran Virginia Coney Island for almost half a century, Van Christoff and his son Craig, are the son and grandson, respectively, of Charlie Christoff, a Macedonian

Virginia Coney Island, one of two historic restaurants on the same block in Jackson, uses the traditional approach of cooking hot dogs in the window to entice hungry customers. *(Photo by Rob Terwilliger)*

immigrant who was one of the first owners of Jackson Coney Island.

The early history of these two East Michigan Avenue coney islands is shrouded in mystery. According to Phil Lazaroff, who owned Jackson Coney from 1999 to 2007, the restaurant was originally started by two Greek men from Detroit, who after a year sold it to Charlie Christoff, his brother Atanas Christoff, and George Todoroff. Jackson city directories show Todoroff operated a restaurant in the mid-1920s on the site that would later become Jackson Coney Island.

No one seems to know who started Virginia Coney Island. Some locals say the restaurant is named after a woman called Virginia, who used to own the place. But others believe the coney island got its name from nearby Virginia Street, which no longer exists.

Jackson and Virginia Coney Islands first appear in the city's directories in 1935. They weren't Jackson's first coney islands. That honor goes to two other downtown restaurants long gone: New York Coney Island and Coney Island Lunch.

Jackson Coney Island has come a long way from the days when it could seat only twelve people at a counter and four tables. Until 1960, the restaurant was located where its parking lot stands today.

Virginia Coney Island has always operated in the same spot, but at some point it expanded into the space next door.

In recent years both coney islands have gained new owners, who have added a few menu items and done a little remodeling but otherwise kept everything the way it's always been.

"It's astonishing every day that we are here how many hot dogs are consumed in Jackson," says Jan Potter, who runs Virginia with her husband, Eli.

The couple, who are Jackson natives and high school sweethearts, had retired from other jobs only to discover a new calling at Virginia. "There are times when it's very demanding," Jan Potter says. "The people are the most amazing part. It's really been quite fun."

Jackson has one of the oldest coney traditions in Michigan.
(Photo by Rob Terwilliger)

The topping makes the coney and, at Jackson Coney Island, owner Lisa Creech makes the topping. People have tried to bribe employees for it. So far, it's still her secret. *(Photo by Rob Terwilliger)*

Beginning to sauce up seven coneys . . .

. . . we have almost all of them . . .

. . . squeeze out the mustard . . .

. . . and finish with onions.
(Photos by Rob Terwilliger)

62

ELI POTTER LISTENS INTENTLY
TO A STORY, ONE OF MANY YOU CAN HEAR EACH DAY
AT A CONEY ISLAND.

VIRGI A
CONEY ISL

Photo by Rob Terwilliger

Lower-Fat Coneys

FOR CONEY DOG LOVERS, IT'S BEST NOT TO THINK ABOUT
CALORIES. BUT FOR THOSE WATCHING THEIR WAISTLINES,
NATIONAL CONEY ISLAND WILLINGLY PROVIDES
A NUTRITIONAL BREAKDOWN OF THEIR CONEYS.

We'll spare you the details, but it's not as horrible as you might think.

"They're better than Big Macs," says Terry Keros of Kerby's Koney Island. Of course, he doesn't recommend gobbling up ten of them each day. "As the ancient Greeks said, 'Moderation in everything,'" Keros advises.

For those desperate for a lower-fat coney dog, there is a solution: turkey coneys. At the Coney Man inside the north atrium of Detroit's New Center One, you can order a coney that comes with a turkey hot dog and wheat bun.

Sales of the turkey coneys started out slow, with only six orders a day. But in recent years these dogs have become more popular, says owner Michael Demerjian.

Different dogs for different folks. Top dog Mike Demerjian (*right*) with (*from left*) Jenna Demerjian, Allie Johnson, and Mike's son, Michael Jr. The Coney Man serves several kinds of coney dogs including a turkey coney dog for the health-conscious and a kosher coney. (*Photo by Paul Hitzelberger*)

A BANNER TELLS HUNGRY DINERS
INSIDE THE ATRIUM OF DETROIT'S NEW CENTER ONE
THAT THEY DON'T EVEN NEED TO GO OUTSIDE
TO GET THEIR FIX.

Photo by Paul Hitzelberger

A fresh coney makes an excellent De-troit how-dee.
Allie Johnson serves one up at the Coney Man at
Detroit's New Center One. *(Photo by Paul Hitzelberger)*

Wesley Gullick is one satisfied-looking customer. He played a cook on the original TV series *Beverly Hills, 90210*. (*Photo by Paul Hitzelberger*)

The Coney Man is a modern incarnation of the original coney island lunch counter. Its setup has an old hot dog wagon appearance. In this case, though, the customers are inside a modern office center, rather than walking up and down the sidewalk looking for a quick bite. Coney island restaurants can be free-standing or inside malls, office buildings, and even gas stations. (*Photo by Paul Hitzelberger*)

Bill's Drive-In

FOR DECADES, BILL'S DRIVE-IN IN YPSILANTI
HAS BEEN MAKING CONEY DOGS ITS OWN UNIQUE WAY.
THE CHILI TOPPING ITS HOT DOGS IS SWEETER
THAN MOST, WITH LESS MEAT.

And the hot dogs are made by Dearborn Sausage using a special recipe from the former Salay Meats in Flint.

The taste draws hordes of Michiganders to Bill's parking lot on the first day of February every year. That's opening day for the bright mustard-colored drive-in, which is closed from November through January.

"The chili really is different. The buns are steamed. The root beer is good. The service is fast," says one loyal fan, Scott Simpson of Brooklyn, Michigan. He's been eating Bill's coney dogs since he was a youngster in the 1960s.

On opening day alone, Bill's usually sells more than two thousand coney dogs. They are served in thin, white paper wrappers, just like in the old days. Most people don't make it out of the parking lot without eating at least two.

The drive-in is named after its founder, William "Bill" Bristol. The business first appeared in Ypsilanti city directories around 1951.

Bill's is now owned by Dan Menna, whose father, Frank, bought the drive-in in 1980 from Bristol's nephew, Paul Adams. Frank Menna delivered hot dog buns to the coney island before he became its owner.

The Mennas have stayed true to Bristol's recipes. "There's never been a reason to change," Dan Menna says. "If it's not broke, don't fix it."

Coney island artwork runs from fanciful Greek scenes to hand-painted murals on cinder-block walls. This is one of the finer cinder-block examples. *(Photo by Bobby Alcott)*

On both ends of this mustard-yellow building, hard by Michigan Avenue, the R in root beer is deliberately tilted, but the coneys are straight-up good. Bill's Drive-In in Ypsilanti doesn't have "coney" in the name, but all it serves are tasty coneys, chips, and strong root beer. *(Photo by Bobby Alcott)*

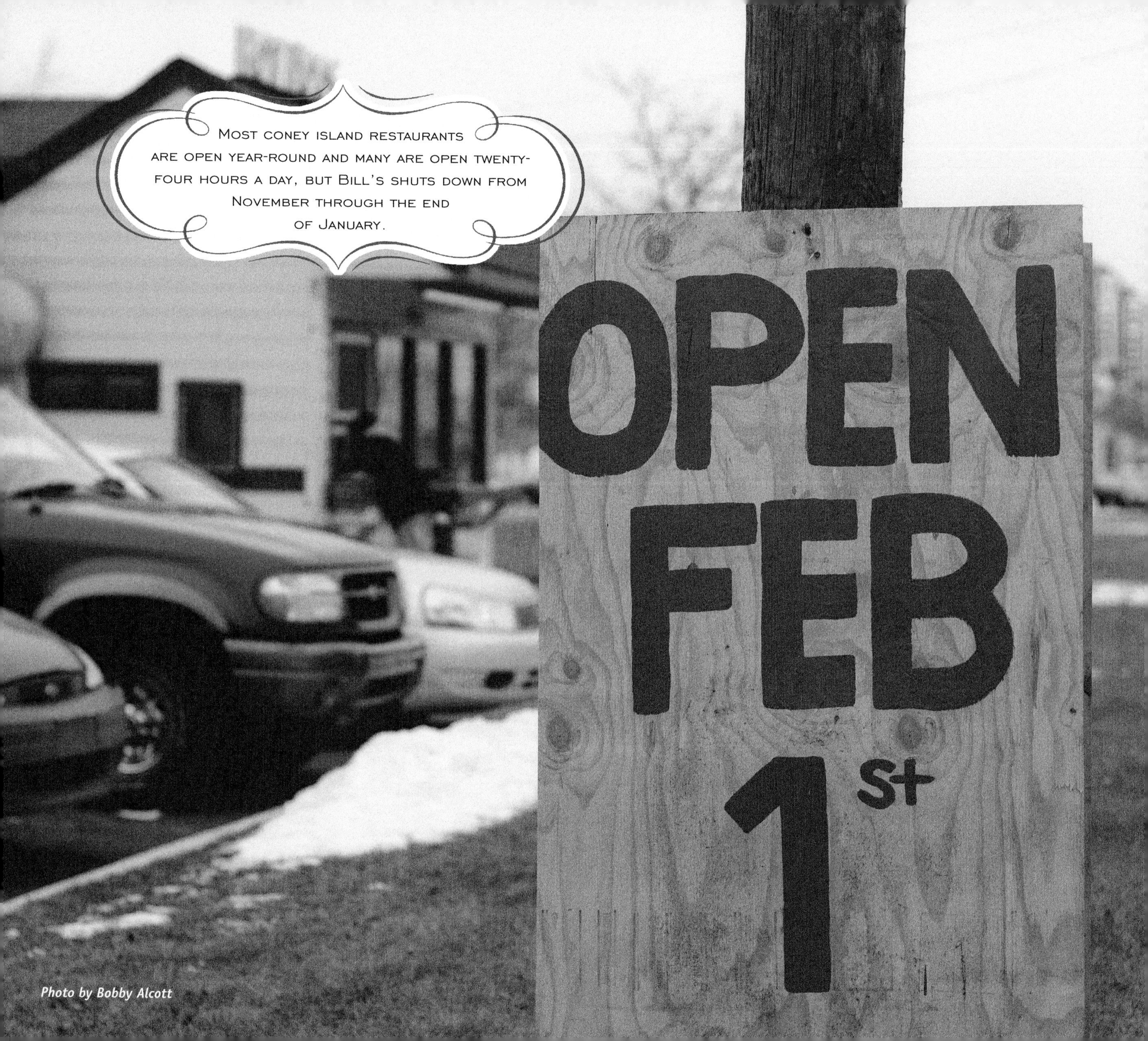

OPEN FEB 1st

Photo by Bobby Alcott

This is one of the very few coney places with car trays. Fans of Bill's Drive-In dine on coneys in their vehicles. There is no inside eating, and coneys taste best when they're hot off the grill. *(Photo by Bobby Alcott)*

George's Senate Coney Islands

A CONEY DOG AND GOLF ANYONE?
GEORGE'S SENATE CONEY ISLAND IN NORTHVILLE, MICHIGAN,
MAY BE ONE OF THE ONLY CONEY ISLANDS
WITH A GOLF COURSE VIEW.

The restaurant is located at the Bushwood Golf Club and looks out on the nine-hole course. Every summer it hosts a few small weddings on its patio. George's refers to owner George Dimopoulos. Like many other Greek immigrants, he discovered that hard work and coneys could lead to the American dream. Today the Northville Senate is one of four metro Detroit coney islands owned by Dimopoulos, a former cook and barber in the Greek army. He also franchises a few other restaurants so it may not be long before Senate becomes Detroit's fourth major coney chain.

Dimopoulos grew up in a small village in southern Greece about five miles away from the Keros family. In 1969, when he was twenty-three, there were few jobs in Greece so he went to join his sister, brother, and other relatives living in Detroit. Dressed in a white shirt and black pants, he arrived in America without speaking any English and with only twenty dollars in his pockets.

Dimopoulos worked in the mornings and evenings at the former Senate Coney Island on Michigan Avenue in Detroit, which his uncle and aunt opened in 1937. In the afternoons, he was a busboy at an upscale restaurant in Detroit.

In those days, Dimopoulos usually did not go home until 3 a.m. One time he worked seventy hours straight, from a Thursday morning to a Sunday morning. In three years he saved $28,000, enough to open his own coney island in Taylor in 1972.

"The first two years were hard," Dimopoulos recalls. "But I never gave up."

Success has not diminished his work ethic. Dimopoulos still shows up at the Northville Senate at 4 a.m. to make his popular lemon rice soup.

Each of his restaurants uses the Senate name, a reference to Detroit's Senate Theatre on Michigan Avenue. At these coney islands, the French fries, mashed potatoes, hash browns, soups, dressings, and rice pudding are all homemade.

But coney dogs are still the main attraction. Customers order three thousand of them every day.

George Dimopoulos, who grew up in Greece and started a small chain of Senate coney islands, lights up a traditional appetizer: saganaki, or kasseri cheese doused in brandy. Opa! (Photo by Bobby Alcott)

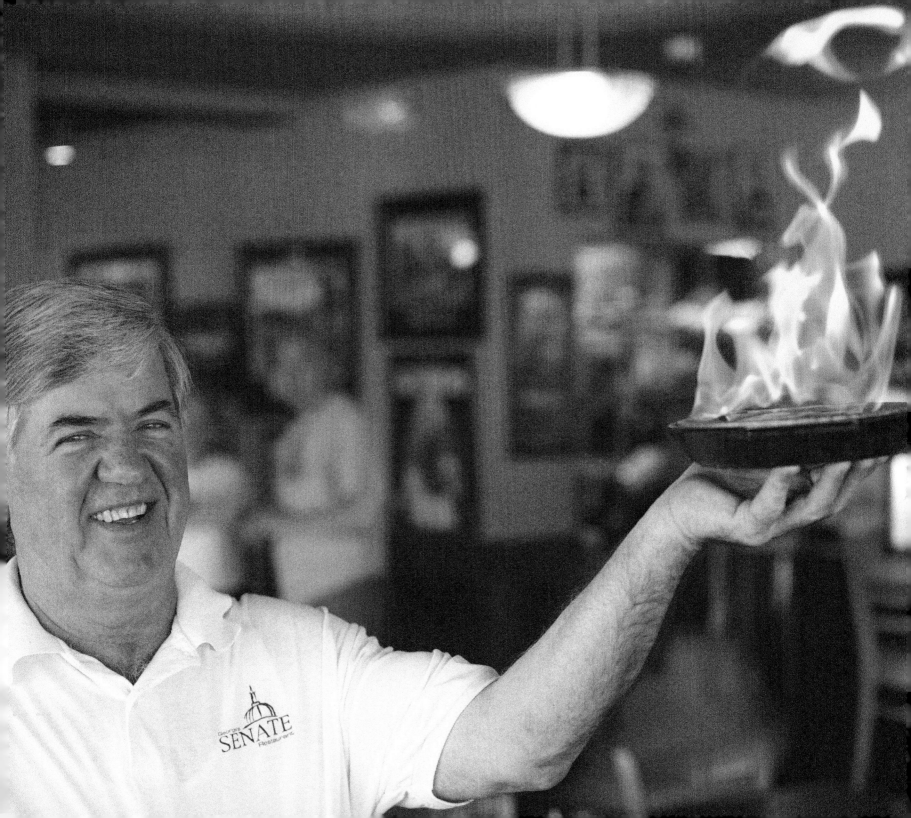

Senate coney islands offer varied menus that can suit any taste or occasion—up to and including wedding receptions. Here are two traditional staples: stuffed grape leaves and a Greek salad. *(Photo by Bobby Alcott)*

Dimopoulos's restaurant in Northville has the unusual distinction of being on a golf course. This happens every time someone yells, "Fore!" *(Photo by Bobby Alcott)*

The Coney Artist

AS IF EATING CONEY DOGS WASN'T SATISFYING ENOUGH,
ONE DETROIT ARTIST HAS TAKEN THE MANIA A STEP FURTHER:
MAKING CONEY ISLAND ART.

Joe Gohl has created more than seven paintings of scenes from Lafayette Coney Island, American Coney Island, National Coney Island, Zeff's Coney Island, and others.

Every time he does a coney painting, people want to buy it, the Dearborn resident says. It's not surprising that coney islands have appealed to this neo-expressionist painter. Gohl has focused his talents on capturing Detroit scenes, from Comerica Park to Eastern Market.

"I love Detroit," he says. "Even today it affords me all kinds of opportunities to paint."

Gohl spent thirty years as a senior graphic artist at General Motors, drawing cars, caricatures of the automaker's executives, and just about anything else. These days, he spends his time working at his studio in the Pioneer Building on East Grand Boulevard. It usually takes him two or three weeks to create a painting.

At coney islands, Gohl looks for colorful characters, something never in short supply. "I've always had fun with my art," he says.

Right at home in his painting, Gohl works at Zeff's and has to fight the temptation to put down the brush and pick up a coney. Later he will work on the painting in his Detroit studio. *(Photo by Bobby Alcott)*

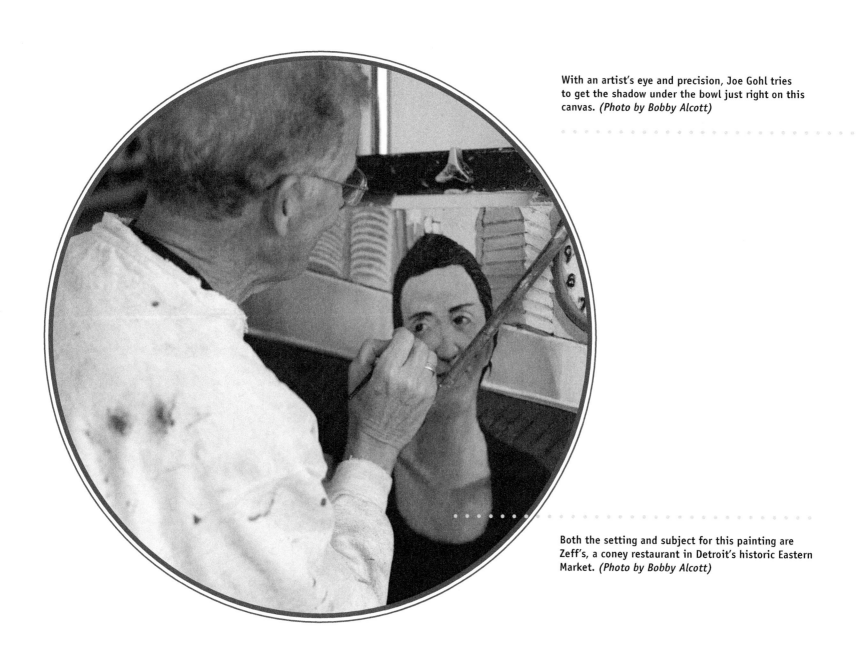

With an artist's eye and precision, Joe Gohl tries to get the shadow under the bowl just right on this canvas. *(Photo by Bobby Alcott)*

Both the setting and subject for this painting are Zeff's, a coney restaurant in Detroit's historic Eastern Market. *(Photo by Bobby Alcott)*

Coney Island Lunch

FOR SOME REASON, CONEY MANIA NEVER TOOK ROOT IN WEST MICHIGAN
THE WAY IT DID IN DETROIT, FLINT, AND JACKSON. STILL, THIS PART
OF THE STATE IS NOT WITHOUT ITS OWN LEGENDARY CONEY ISLAND—
CONEY ISLAND LUNCH IN DOWNTOWN KALAMAZOO.

The restaurant is one of the state's oldest coney islands. According to owner Bill Adams, Greek immigrant Gus Marinos opened Coney Island Lunch in 1915. He sold it in 1933 to another Greek immigrant, Adams's father, Frank. Today two of Bill Adams's three sons help out at the family business.

Coney Island Lunch serves Flint-style coney dogs, making the meat topping from scratch. The recipe, which Bill Adams believes came from Marinos, has never changed, good news for the five generations of coney lovers who regularly come through the restaurant's doors.

At Coney Island Lunch, the past has become an integral part of the present. It uses the same hot dog grill that the restaurant had when Frank Adams bought the place. The tables, chairs, and stools are also original, though they have been refurbished. And the mosaic on the floor at the front of the coney island dates from the 1950s.

A few things, of course, have been altered. Bill Adams has expanded the menu. And a machine has taken over the job of chopping the two hundred pounds of white onions that top the restaurant's coney dogs every week.

But one thing will never change: its focus on quality. Coney Island Lunch uses choice ground round and takes pride in the taste of its French fries. "My dad was really quality conscious," Bill Adams says.

Grilled up in a sunny window with the meat topping warming beside them, these coneys will go down in a hurry. *(Photo by Rob Terwilliger)*

Coney Island Lunch has been serving residents in Kalamazoo since 1915. Many longtime coney island restaurants came into business as lunch counters. Kalamazoo is 140 miles west of downtown Detroit. Steve Adams *(left)* and his father, Bill Adams *(right)*. Bill owns the coney island and Steve works with his father. *(Photo by Rob Terwilliger)*

No coney is complete without onions, like these at the Coney Island Lunch. White onions seem to be most common, but coney places diverge as to whether to chop the onions by hand or machine. Some say machines mash the onions. *(Photo by Rob Terwilliger)*

Steve Adams spoons meat topping onto hot dogs, which have already been squirted with mustard. WMD—Ways of Mustard Delivery—can be either squeeze bottles or spoons, but you need a spoon or ladle for the meat. *(Photo by Rob Terwilliger)*

ONE ORDER OF CHILI FRIES—
A CONEY ISLAND STAPLE—COMING UP. EMPLOYEE
CHARLES KAISER DOES THE HONORS.

Photo by Rob Terwilliger

MAMA VICKI'S
CONEY ISLAND

Mama Vicki's Coney Islands

IN PORT HURON, MICHIGAN, CONEY DOGS COME WITH A
SLIGHTLY DIFFERENT TWIST. THE BEANLESS CHILI GOES ON TOP
OF THE MUSTARD AND ONIONS, INSTEAD OF THE OTHER WAY AROUND,
AND THE HOT DOGS ARE SKINLESS.

This "over the top" chili may sound like coney heresy, but that's the way it's been done for decades at Coney Island Lunch, now called Mama Vicki's Coney Island. It's one of the oldest coney islands in Michigan.

The downtown Port Huron restaurant was started by a Greek immigrant in 1917, according to Effie Janis. Her late husband, Jim, and his brother, Gus, bought the coney island in 1924 and continued using the original owner's chili recipe, a tradition that carries on today.

In the mid-1960s, Coney Island Lunch moved up Huron Avenue to its present location. At the restaurant's grand reopening, customers lined up around the block to buy thousands of coney dogs at the special yesteryear price of a nickel each.

After the deaths of her husband and brother-in-law, Effie Janis kept the business going until she sold it in 1976 to Christopher Pozios, another Greek immigrant. Pozios had learned the coney business at downtown Detroit's American Coney Island, where he worked for almost twenty years.

Pozios did well. His two sons, Bill and Evans, now also run two other coney islands in Fort Gratiot and Macomb Township.

A few years ago they decided to rename their trio of restaurants in honor of their late mother, whom some customers at the Coney Island Lunch affectionately called "Mama Vicki." She made the chili.

At its three locations, Mama Vicki's makes coney dogs that are "over the top": the chili goes on after the mustard and onions. We asked if we could get one the regular way, with the onions and mustard on top, and they told us no. We liked that. *(Photo by Brett J. Lawrence)*

Mama Vicki died in 2003. Her husband, Chris, and their sons, Evans and Bill, have dedicated the business, which began as one restaurant called Coney Island Lunch, to her memory. *(Photo by Brett J. Lawrence)*

Chris Pozios and one of his sons, Bill, who looks after the
Fort Gratiot restaurant, their second, which opened in 1991.
(Photo by Brett J. Lawrence)

One of Michigan's oldest coney islands, it has roots that go back even before the 1923 on its awning. Port Huron just doesn't get the notice of Flint or Detroit. *(Photo by Brett J. Lawrence)*

This is the order of toppings at Mama Vicki's: mustard, onions, chili sauce last. *(Photo by Brett J. Lawrence)*

House of Doggs

IT'S THE ULTIMATE FACEOFF—DETROIT-STYLE CONEY DOGS
VERSUS FLINT-STYLE ONES IN NEUTRAL TERRITORY.
THAT'S WHAT HAPPENS EVERY JANUARY AND FEBRUARY
AT HOUSE OF DOGGS IN DOWNTOWN TRAVERSE CITY.

To add some excitement during these slow winter months, the hot dog haven keeps a scorecard of sales of the "Motowns," the Detroit coneys, and its Flint coneys, which it calls "Grand Funks."

At the first showdown in 2007, "the Motown dogs blew away the Grand Funks," House of Doggs owner Nick McAllister says. But Flint coney fans shouldn't lose hope. The gap has been getting closer in recent years.

Though House of Doggs sells eighteen different kinds of hot dogs, two-thirds of its sales are Motowns and Grand Funks. The chili and meat topping for these dogs are McAllister's creations.

Year-round, the Detroit-style coney dogs are the most popular, followed by the Chicago dogs and the Grand Funks. As for McAllister, he won't choose between Detroit and Flint coney dogs, saying he likes them equally. However, his real love is for another dog on the menu, the Jazz. It comes loaded with chili, Chicago fire mustard, Cholula hot sauce, jalapeno, banana pepper, onion, and celery salt.

The H.O.D. amuses diners with huge graphic murals and eclectic decorations. The rolls of paper towels are just for cleanup. (Photo by E. Terry Clark)

With its outside tables and a summery day, Traverse City's House of Doggs in northern Michigan looks as though it could be a Parisian café. (Photo by E. Terry Clark)

Owner Nick McAllister has collected a variety of coney and hot dog recipes from around the state and country. *(Photo by E. Terry Clark)*

It is about 190 miles from H.O.D. to Flint and another 60 miles to Detroit, but you can get both tastes on the same tray here. *(Photo by E. Terry Clark)*

H.O.D. Menu

MOTOWN	Chili, Onion, Mustard	2.69
Rock	Chili, Cheese, Ketchup, Mustard, Pickle, Onion	2.89
COUNTRY	Chili, Ketchup, Mustard, Pickle, Onion	2.89
R&B	Chili, Sauerkraut, Ketchup, Mustard, Pickle, Onion	2.89
Reggae	Sauerkraut, Pickle, Mustard	2.89
Re-Bop	Ketchup, Mustard	2.15
BLUES	Chili, Cheese	2.89
Salsa	Chili, Jalapeno, Louisiana Hot Sauce, Onion, Celery Salt	2.89
JAZZ	Chili, Chicago Fire Mustard, Cholula Hot Sauce, Jalapeno, Banana Pepper, Onion, Celery Salt	2.89
MARIACHI	Relish, Onion, Tomato, Sour Cream	2.89
Honky Tonk		

H.O.D. Menu

GRAND FUNK	Flint Coney Sauce, Mustard, Onions	2.69
DISCO	Sweet Pickle Relish Ketchup, Mustard	2.15
CHICAGO	Tomato, Pickle, Onion, Sport Pepper, Mustard, Celery Salt	2.89
HOD FUSION	H.O.D. Dip, Ketchup, Mustard, Crushed Potato Chips	2.89
SOUTHERN ROCK	Coleslaw, Ketchup, Mustard	2.89
Alternative	Sauerkraut, Cheese, Ketchup, Mustard, Pickle, Onion, No Dog	2.69
POLKA	Polish Sausage, Sauerkraut	3.5

Extra's

TECHNO Dog	Corn Dog	2
H.O.D. Brat	Original, Cheese or Cherry	3
H.O.D. Hamburger	Add Cheese .25	

MIX-AND-MATCH VARIATIONS
INSPIRED BY DETROIT, FLINT, CHICAGO, AND OTHER
PLACES. H.O.D. GOES IN FOR MUSICAL NAMES.

Beyond the Coney Dog

IN METRO DETROIT, THE ENTHUSIASM FOR CONEY DOGS HAS SPILLED OVER INTO OTHER FOODS. CONEY TACOS AND CONEY FRIES ARE THE MOST POPULAR CONEY DOG SPINOFFS, BUT YOU CAN ALSO FIND CONEY PIZZAS, CONEY WRAPS, CONEY BURGERS, CONEY SLIDERS, AND CONEY OMELETTES.

Some coney islands have even created their own twists on the coney dog by making them with kielbasas or spicy hot dogs or sausages. And in Dearborn, many coney islands sell halal coney dogs.

To find what works, all you need is a little imagination and a willingness to experiment. That's what happened at Pete's Coney Island II in Clarkston. More than a dozen years ago, the restaurant invented "Pete's-Za Coney Lover's Personal Pizza"—coney chili, hot dog slices, chopped onion, mustard, and melted mozzarella and cheddar cheese on a grilled pita crust.

"We just thought we would try something different," said owner Ed Zull. Over the years, the coney island has kept the pizza the same. But Zull has noticed that some customers like to personalize it even more, adding things like sauerkraut, sour cream, jalapeno peppers, relish, and mayonnaise.

Ed Zull, owner of Pete's Coney Island II in Clarkston, serves up a "Pete's-Za Coney Lover's Personal Pizza" and two with everything. *(Photo by Bobby Alcott)*

This is the Angelo's Coney Island version of the coney taco, called the hard-shell coney, with Flint-style meat topping. This version has a hot dog, meat topping, and onions. *(Photo by Bobby Alcott)*

Why is this man putting meat sauce on taco chips? He is making the Pete's II version of a coney taco. Some versions start with flatbread. Many then go up with tomatoes, lettuce, onions, and shredded cheese. *(Photo by Bobby Alcott)*

A "Pete's-Za," up close and personal. A similar dish was on the menu at a restaurant in Detroit and named after a Detroit Free Press columnist who regularly extolled coneys. *(Photo by Bobby Alcott)*

Outside Michigan

THE PLEASURES OF A CONEY DOG CAN BE FOUND OUTSIDE MICHIGAN,
BUT YOU HAVE TO LOOK A LOT HARDER FOR THEM. NOT ALL STATES
HAVE CONEY ISLANDS AND WHEN THEY DO, IT'S USUALLY ONLY
ONE OR TWO RESTAURANTS.

But don't dismiss these out-of-state coney dogs. Some of them are a treat, even if they aren't made with Michigan hot dogs. So the next time you're traveling, try to find a coney island. You might be surprised by what you discover.

Here are two not to be missed.

George's Coney Island, Worcester, Massachusetts

You can see George's sign from miles away, before you even come near this coney island about an hour west of Boston. The fifty-foot-tall art deco sign from the 1940s shows several fingers gripping a coney dog with drops of mustard falling off.

The fingers were modeled after those of George Tsagarelis, this coney island's former owner. He came to the United States in 1916 from Greece and bought this downtown Worcester restaurant in 1927 from another Greek immigrant. Legend has it that the business, which has also been called Coney Island Lunch, opened in 1918.

Tsagarelis expanded the coney island, which has become a favorite gathering spot for locals. It usually sells a thousand coney dogs a day except on Tuesdays when the restaurant is closed. George's is self-serve, so customers line up at the front counter to buy their Flint-style coneys, saying "two up" just like in Michigan.

George's Coney Island in Worcester, Massachusetts, dates back to 1918. It was started by a Greek immigrant. *(Photo by Christine Dunshee Peterson)*

JOSH HOLDEN SENDS A BUN BY AIR. CONEY ISLAND HOT DOG PRODUCTION IS AN ASSEMBLY-LINE OPERATION AND SPEED IS APPRECIATED WHEN ONE IS HUNGRY.

The secret recipe for George's homemade meat topping came from the coney island's original owner. Unlike in Michigan, George's uses a skinless hot dog.

Like other old-fashioned coney islands, George's has tried to keep things the way they have always been. Though the coat hooks are gone, the original counter has been replaced, and an internet jukebox was added, the layout of the restaurant and its floor haven't changed at all. Customers still munch on their coney dogs while sitting in high-backed wood booths with their fading reddish-orange tables. Over the years, coney lovers have written their names on the booths, tables, and walls.

Tsagarelis died in 1980. George's is now run by Tsagarelis's son-in-law, Solon Tsandikos; his granddaughter, Kathryn Tsandikos; and her husband, Andrew Kelleher.

Unlike Michigan coney island restaurants, the one in Worcester serves skinless wieners. *(Photo by Christine Dunshee Peterson)*

Kathryn Tsandikos during a lull in action. Customers line up at the counter and collect their coneys as they pass along. *(Photo by Christine Dunshee Peterson)*

Kathryn Tsandikos says customers still remember her grandfather cutting hot dog links at the counter. That was back in the days when hot dogs came in strips that were thirty or forty feet long.

"It's a feel-good kind of place," she says of her family's coney island. "Everybody loves hot dogs."

Coney Island Sandwich Shop, St. Petersburg, Florida

Locals simply call it "Coney Island" and there's a reason they keep coming back year after year. Owner Hank Barlas and his staff know how to make delicious Flint-style coney dogs. One is not enough.

A hungry diner pulls up to a stool at the frozen-in-time Coney Island Sandwich Shop in St. Petersburg, Florida, ready for a meal and the latest gossip. *(Photo by Brian Blanco)*

The classic Coca-Cola signs and the awning give St. Pete's premier coney island emporium a look of permanence. *(Photo by Brian Blanco)*

Sitting at the counter of this coney island is almost like taking a step back in time. One of the oldest restaurants in St. Petersburg, Coney Island uses an old-fashioned cash register and a refrigerator built in the World War II era. No menus are available, but newcomers can see what's cooking on the white menu board hanging on one of the walls. This is the type of restaurant that still makes milkshakes by hand.

"Old-time customers don't want me to change anything," Barlas says.

His father, Peter, opened Coney Island in 1926. Hank Barlas isn't sure if it started out as a coney island but the restaurant was originally at a different location, near the intersection of Central and 9th streets. When Peter Barlas split with his partners, he moved the business to what is now Coney Island's parking lot.

Like other coney pioneers, Peter Barlas left his native Greece to move to the United States, working in Boston and Virginia before settling in St. Petersburg.

In Coney Island's early days, 9th Street was paved with red bricks and trolley cars regularly rumbled by. Back then, air conditioning was just a novelty so Florida didn't have many tourists in the summer. Since the locals usually left town, Peter Barlas would take a break from selling coney dogs to head to New Jersey to sell fruits and vegetables from a truck.

At one point, he got sick from tuberculosis and almost lost his coney island. He had leased the restaurant to someone who took his money and he had to work hard to reestablish his credit with suppliers.

This isn't *Cheers*, it's not a bar, and those guys aren't Cliff and Norm. But you get the feeling that this is the kind of place where everyone knows your name. **(Photo by Brian Blanco)**

People who eat at the Coney Island Sandwich Shop can get anything on the menu and, as one newspaper said, a side of sass. **(Photo by Brian Blanco)**

Peter Barlas died in 1983 but not before warning his two sons, Hank and George, to keep his coney recipe a secret. The meat topping is made from scratch, using ground beef, not beef hearts.

The two brothers operated the coney island together for many years until George Barlas died in 2005.

On a good day, Coney Island sells six hundred coney dogs. It has several longtime employees who give the place much of its character. One of them was former dishwasher Danny Murphy, who lost his battle with cancer in 2002 after working at the coney island for twenty-six years. A painting of him hangs on the restaurant's back wall.

"It's a neat place," says Gail Kelley, who has worked as a waitress at Coney Island for more than eighteen years. "I have fun with my customers."

Though Coney Island still doesn't sell French fries, in 2009 it added Barq's root beer to its menu, the first new item in fifty years.

Two with everything, just made and ready to go out to a customer at this coney island opened by its Greek founder, Peter Barlas, in 1926. *(Photo by Brian Blanco)*

Slight adjustments to the gas under the grill ensure that anyone coming through the door can be served within minutes of ordering. *(Photo by Brian Blanco)*

〜〜〜

103

SURROUNDED BY THE CHIPS, POP, AND JERSEYS HE LEFT IN DETROIT, AS WELL AS THE SLOGANS AND SIGNATURES OF PEOPLE WHO LOVE THIS PLACE, MANNY SANCHEZ CAN STILL FEEL RIGHT AT HOME IN VEGAS.

PLEASE PAY WHEN ORDERING

Photo by Bobby Alcott

Detroit Motor City Coney Island

THE PASSION FOR CONEY DOGS RUNS SO DEEP
THAT ONE EX-DETROITER HAS EVEN BROUGHT THEM
TO THE DESERT. LITERALLY.

In downtown Henderson, Nevada, a short drive southeast of the Las Vegas strip, Emanuel "Manny" Sanchez operates Detroit Motor City Coney Island.

Don't let the palm trees outside this small restaurant fool you. Though it may look worlds away from the streets of Detroit, this coney island offers locals, Michigan transplants, and Las Vegas tourists a taste of the real thing: coney dogs just like they make them in the Motor City.

Sanchez buys his hot dogs directly from Dearborn Sausage and his chili from National Chili Company. And the white onions he uses are chopped by hand.

The restaurant's building doesn't allow grills so this coney island's hot dogs are cooked in the oven and then steamed.

"There's something about the chili and those dogs. They are addictive," says Sanchez, who grew up in southwest Detroit and moved to Las Vegas in 1997.

Restaurant founder Manny Sanchez wears his airline mechanic's uniform—an emblem of the job that got him transferred from Detroit to Las Vegas—to serve customers. *(Photo by Bobby Alcott)*

For Michiganders tired of the neon lights, crowds, and buffets on the strip, stepping into this coney island reminds them of why they yearn for home. Its walls and ceilings are adorned with jerseys, T-shirts, banners, and stickers touting the Red Wings, the Detroit Lions, and the Detroit Pistons. Here you can find old photos of Bob-Lo boats, the Model T, and Greenfield Village, among others.

To complete the homage to Detroit, this coney island sells all kinds of Faygo pop, Vernors ginger ale, Better Made potato chips, and Sanders hot fudge sauce. Visitors can even sign their names on the restaurant's white walls.

"People bring in Michigan stuff all the time," says Sanchez's mother, Patty Batwinas, who helps her son run the place.

A sports fanatic, Sanchez got the idea for opening his coney island while watching the Pistons play. He spent almost a month doing research and meeting with suppliers, sitting many hours at the Lafayette Coney Island, his favorite.

"We ate a lot of coney dogs growing up," Sanchez says. "I missed that food."

At first business was slow because no one knew about the coney island. Sanchez spent more than a year pounding the streets, putting fliers on cars. But the hard work paid off. Detroit Motor City Coney Island has gained a following, especially among those already familiar with the pleasures of devouring a coney dog.

"This is all mine," Sanchez says. "I'm proud of it. I really believe in this."

If Sanchez gets his way, expect Detroit Motor City Coney Island to open a second location in the Las Vegas area.

The Big Three take on a whole new meaning two thousand miles from Detroit. *(Photo by Ryan Southen)*

Two with everything can teleport you from the desert to the D. Manny Sanchez's mother, Patty Batwinas, helps her son run the place. *(Photo by Ryan Southen)*

Pop—that's what we call it in Michigan, not soda—lines the shelves at Detroit Motor City Coney Island in Henderson, Nevada. And that is Faygo pop, traditional Detroit stuff. *(Photo by Bobby Alcott)*

Neon, Neon in the Night

MANY OF THE BEST CONEY ISLAND RESTAURANTS ARE OPEN
TWENTY-FOUR HOURS A DAY. NOTHING SAYS "OPEN ALL NIGHT" LIKE
BRIGHT NEON, WHETHER IT'S A SIMPLE SIGN IN A STEAMY WINDOW
OR A BEACON LOOMING HIGH OVERHEAD.

When other restaurants around them are cold and closed, coney islands are warm, steamy places where you can get a quick bite and people won't hassle you to hurry back out into the night.

Some of the finest examples of the neon sign maker's art illuminate the skies outside coney island restaurants. They are beacons to travelers and out-late-at-nighters, telling them that yes, we're open, and there is good stuff inside.

Running a coney island can be a hard life, and staying open twenty-four hours just adds to that. But some traditionalists believe that if the door is ever locked, it is not a coney island in the truest sense.

Athens Coney Island's architecture and location along M-1, Woodward Avenue, has made it a natural headquarters for the Woodward Dream Cruise classic car parade. Woodward Avenue is home to a dozen coney islands, but other streets have more. *(Photo by Rob Terwilliger)*

Plain and simple at the Coney Island Sandwich Shop in St. Petersburg, Florida. Come on in! *(Photo by Brian Banco)*

National Coney Island marketing includes bright lights, a website, monthly specials, and a mascot, Mr. Pop—available as a bobble-head doll.

Neon mustard drips from the George's Coney Island sign in Worcester, Massachusetts. The fingers were fashioned after one of the hands of former owner George Tsagarelis. *(Photo by Christine Dunshee Peterson)*

In Flint, Starlite Coney Island's overhead constellation makes it an attraction—and validates its name. *(Photo by Bobby Alcott)*

The Last Bite

NEW YORK AND CHICAGO ARE TOPS WHEN IT COMES TO PIZZA.
BOSTON CAN BOAST ABOUT ITS LOBSTER AND CLAM CHOWDER.
AND YOU CAN'T VISIT NEW ORLEANS WITHOUT SAMPLING
ITS CAJUN CUISINE.

But nowhere in the world can match Detroit and Michigan when it comes to coney dogs. With each new decade, demand for these tasty concoctions has grown stronger, as evidenced by the many coney island restaurants opening in the state every year.

The coney story is not just a celebration of food. It's a tribute to the men and women who work at hundreds of coney islands in Michigan and other states who keep the coney tradition alive. These are the people who toil long hours, slicing thousands of onions by hand and making batch after batch of their special beanless chili or meat topping.

Day after day. Year after year.

For some, coney islands turned out to be their ticket to the American dream, affording them a way of life they never dreamed possible. For others, it's about making a living doing something they love.

As the coney dog prepares to enter its second century, the beloved hot dog is poised to win the hearts and stomachs of new generations. Culinary trends may come and go, but Detroit's signature food has proven that its appeal is timeless.

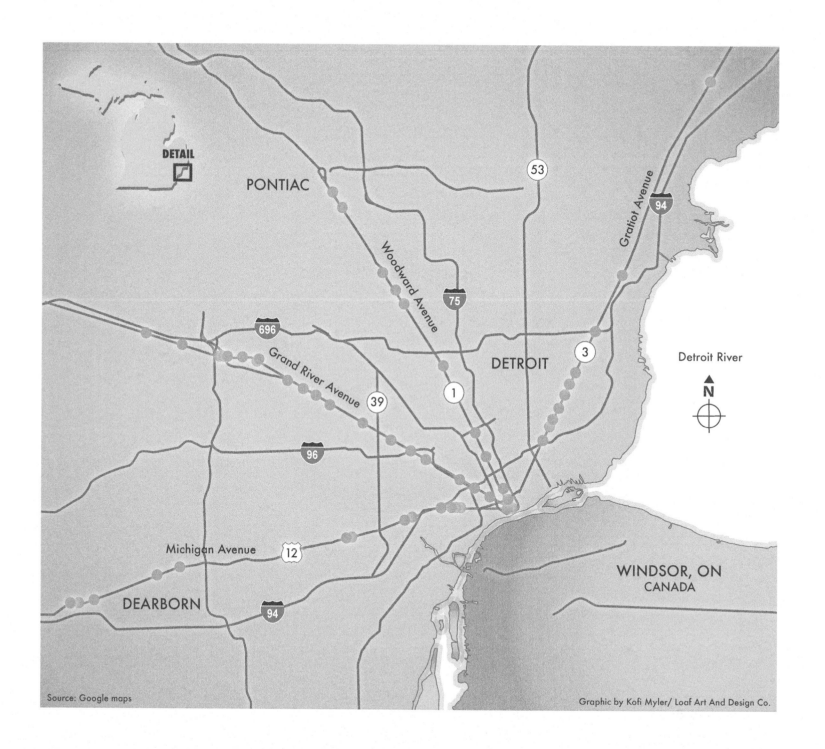

PONTIAC

DETAIL

Woodward Avenue

Gratiot Avenue

53

94

696

Grand River Avenue

DETROIT

39

1

3

Detroit River

N

96

Michigan Avenue

12

WINDSOR, ON
CANADA

DEARBORN

94

You're Never Far from a Coney

How many coney island restaurants are there in the Detroit area? Who knows? Some of the best don't even have "coney island" in their names. And many, many restaurants that serve coneys cannot properly be called coney islands. New coneys are opening and old ones are closing all the time. But there are a lot. Hundreds.

To give you an idea of how many there are, we drove along four of Detroit's main avenues, just looking for coney islands.

When we saw one, we stopped, jumped out, and checked the place out. We ate at many of them, but not all.

There are even more coney islands between these streets than there are along them. Detroit has countless coneys. Let's leave it at that.

We found more than 60 coney islands along just these four avenues. Here they are, listed from downtown and traveling out the spokes of the Motor City:

Michigan Avenue

American Coney Island, 114 West Lafayette Boulevard, Detroit

Lafayette Coney Island, 118 West Lafayette Boulevard, Detroit

Onassis Coney Island, 1501 Michigan Avenue, Detroit, MI

Zorba's Restaurant & Coney Island, 5517 Michigan Avenue, Detroit

Adi's Coney Island, 6171 Michigan Avenue, Detroit

George's Famous Coney Island, 6362 Michigan Avenue, Detroit

Michigan Coney Island, 7506 Michigan Avenue, Detroit

Joe's Top Dog Coney Island, 13342 Michigan Avenue, Dearborn

Avenue Coney & Grill, 14456 Michigan Avenue, Dearborn

Cedars Coney Island, 22443 Michigan Avenue, Dearborn

Holiday Grill Coney Island, 22926 Michigan Avenue, Dearborn

L. George's Coney Island Restaurant, 34438 Michigan Avenue, Wayne

L. George's Coney Island Restaurant, 43711 Michigan Avenue, Canton

Village Coney Island, 47182 Michigan Avenue, Canton

Bill's Drive-In, 1292 East Michigan Avenue, Ypsilanti

Luca's Coney Island & Restaurant, 309 East Michigan Avenue, Ypsilanti

Abe's Coney Island & Restaurant, 402 West Michigan Avenue, Ypsilanti

Mark's Midtown Coney Island, 529 East Michigan Avenue, Saline

Grand River Avenue

United Café, 3641 Grand River Avenue, Detroit

Allstar Café, 5270 Grand River Avenue, Detroit

Apollo Coney Island, 7635 Grand River Avenue, Detroit

Hollywood Coney Island, 12033 Grand River Avenue, Detroit

Galaxy Coney Island, 13611 Grand River Avenue, Detroit

Universal Coney Island, 15951 Grand River Avenue, Detroit

Hollywood Coney Island, 20240 Grand River Avenue, Detroit

Royal Coney Island, 24480 Grand River Avenue, Detroit

Hefty's Coney Island 26080 Grand River Avenue, Redford

L. George's Coney Island, 27434 Grand River Avenue, Livonia

Col's Place Coney Island, 29420 Grand River Avenue, Farmington Hills

Tina's Coney Island, 23310 Grand River Avenue, Farmington

Dmitri's Coney Island, 33200 Grand River Avenue, Farmington

Plato's Coney Island, 35227 Grand River Avenue, Farmington

Yesterday's Coney Island, 37125 Grand River Avenue, Farmington

L. George's Coney Island, 24250 Grand River Avenue, Farmington Hills

Great Lakes Coney Island, 38425 Grand River Avenue, Farmington Hills

Athenian Coney Island, Grand River Avenue at
Novi Road, Novi

Leo's Coney Island, 40380 Grand River Avenue,
Novi

Leo's Coney Island, 47830 Grand River Avenue,
Novi

Woodward Avenue

Woodward Coney Island, 616 Woodward Avenue,
Detroit

Leo's Coney Island at Comerica Park

Detroit One Coney Island, 3433 Woodward
Avenue, Detroit

Aloha Coney Island, 8444 Woodward Avenue,
Detroit

Classic Café Coney Island, 12857 Woodward
Avenue, Highland Park

Mr. Coney Island, 14467 Woodward Avenue,
Highland Park

Hambo Coney Island, 22900 Woodward Avenue,
Royal Oak

Leo's in Northwood Mall at Woodward and 13 Mile
Road, Royal Oak

Athens Coney Island, 32657 Woodward Avenue,
Royal Oak

Spangas Coney Island Plus, 32867 Woodward
Avenue, Royal Oak

Leo's Coney Island, 154 South Old Woodward
Avenue, Birmingham

Kerby's in Kingswood Plaza, northwest corner of
Woodward Avenue and Square Lake Road,
Bloomfield

Bloomfield Coney Island and Restaurant, 732
Woodward Avenue, Bloomfield

Gratiot Avenue

Hollywood Coney Island, 9951 Gratiot Avenue,
Detroit

Aloha Coney Café, 10993 Gratiot Avenue, Detroit

Olympia Coney Island, 11999 Gratiot Avenue,
Detroit

Coney Time Coney Island, 13240 Gratiot Avenue,
Detroit

V.I.P. Coney Island, 14300 Gratiot Avenue, Detroit

Embassy Coney Island, 14987 Gratiot Avenue,
Detroit

Western Coney & Grill, 21515 Gratiot Avenue,
Eastpointe

National Coney Island, 27027 Gratiot Avenue,
Roseville

Kerby's Koney Island, 33812 Gratiot Avenue,
Clinton

Coney Island, USA, 50800 Gratiot Avenue,
Chesterfield Township

Gus's Coney Island, 50899 Gratiot Avenue,
Chesterfield Township

New Haven Coney Island, 57550 Gratiot Avenue,
New Haven

Contributors

Katherine Yung is a reporter at the *Detroit Free Press* covering Michigan's economy and other business subjects. Before joining the *Free Press* in May 2007, she worked for the *Dallas Morning News* and the *Detroit News*. Katherine is a graduate of Brown University and Columbia University's Graduate School of Journalism. Her love for all things coney was inspired by her husband, Rick Fischer, who introduced her to the delicious dogs at American Coney Island many years ago.

Joe Grimm is a lifelong Detroiter and a member of the advisory board for the Great Lakes Books Series at Wayne State University Press. Following a thirty-one-year newspaper career, twenty-five of them spent at the *Detroit Free Press*, he became a journalism professor at Michigan State University. He teaches, writes, edits, and provides journalism career advice. He likes to try new coney island restaurants and loves to take visitors out for a side-by-side taste challenge at American and Lafayette downtown.

A dozen photographers, led by Bobby Alcott and Ted Fines of EXPOSURE.Detroit, worked on this book. Photographers in Florida and Massachusetts were brought in to help. Their varied approaches to photography give Coney Detroit its snap.

Bobby Alcott is an award-winning professional photographer based in Royal Oak, Michigan. Mostly known for his destination weddings, Bobby's work has taken him around the globe and has appeared in books and magazines worldwide. Bobby is also the founder and chairman of EXPOSURE.Detroit, a not-for-profit photography club with almost two thousand members, and in 2010 was selected as one of Detroit's Top Five Photographers for the second consecutive year. A graduate of Michigan State University, his life-long love of coneys led him to help photograph this project, which in turn has helped feed his soul—as well as his stomach. You can see his work at www.bobbyalcott.com.

Brian Blanco is a freelance photojournalist and commercial photographer in the Tampa Bay area. A self-proclaimed expert on cheap Florida motels, Brian enjoys mopeds, late-evening light, and any food that gets handed out of a window. He is a member of the team awarded the 2006 Pulitzer Prize Gold Medal for Public Service for coverage of Hurricane Katrina.

Keith Burgess, born in Detroit in 1973, is a self-taught artist. Pursuing photography since the age of twenty-eight, he has won the Center for Railroad Photography and Art's Creative Photography Gold Award in 2007 and 2009, and has been exhibited at the Alden B. Dow Museum of Art and Science in Midland, Michigan. Burgess strives to reveal the underlying emotion of what he describes as otherwise "everyday mundane objects." The images in his series "Portrait of the American Landscape" and "Architecture of Decline" convey solitude, sadness, loss, and longing.

E. Terry Clark was born and raised in Dearborn, Michigan. He graduated from the University of Michigan and lived in Ann Arbor for many years before moving to Traverse City in 1974. He retired from an architectural practice in 2002, got his first single-lens-reflex digital camera that year, and developed a very serious interest in photography. He spends most of his free time photographing northern Michigan along with his wife.

Ted Fines was born in Toronto, Canada, and currently resides in Grosse Pointe, Michigan. Ted's award-winning photography has been featured in books and magazines, as well as in several gallery shows since 2005. The Wayne State University graduate was an original member of EXPOSURE.Detroit.

Paul Hitzelberger is a Michigan-based freelance photographer dedicated to capturing images around the city of Detroit and the Midwest. Growing up in a family of avid recreational photographers unknowingly drew him to the hobby and love of the art. Paul has photographed many places in the Motor City that scream of its past and future, some rare, some obvious, but all with an unparalleled uniqueness and passion for Michigan and photography. You can see his work at www.paulhitzphotography.com.

Brett J. Lawrence resides in Warren, Michigan. He is an artist by education, a graphic designer by trade, but it's photography that he is most passionate about. A diehard fan of the true coney, he and his family have a tradition of eating coneys on Christmas Day in a Detroit diner. He challenges you to guess which one. His work can be viewed online at www.lawrencecreative.net.

Eric Peoples is the founder of EPic Images, LLC, based in Royal Oak, Michigan, and in operation since 2008. Eric offers distinctive, professional portrait, fashion and glamor, wedding, and event photography. He is also a founding member of the Detroit Studio Collective, a photography co-op comprised of several local working photographers. EPic Images can be found on the web at www.epicimagesonline.com.

Christine Dunshee Peterson studied photography at Fitchburg State College under Peter Laytin and graduated in 1988. After college, she worked for a white-water rafting photo company in Maine, shooting stills and video of rafting enthusiasts. That gave way to a job at a weekly newspaper, then as a biomedical photographer at UMass Medical Center in the department of cell biology. After five years there, she landed at the Worcester *Telegram & Gazette*. Favorite assignments include wild animals, farming, live music, horses, car shows, children, theater, baseball—and neon.

Ryan Southen is a photographer living in metro Detroit who specializes in contemporary wedding photography as well as architectural photography. You can see his wedding work at www.ryansouthen.com and his architectural work at www.ryansouthenphotography.com.

Spike has called Michigan home since the late '90s. His photography has appeared in local art galleries, national magazines, and college textbooks. His other creative release is his day job: co-host of the Mojo in the Morning radio show on Channel 955 (WKQI-FM , 95.5). Spike likes his coney with chili and onion.

Rob Terwilliger is a wedding and portrait photographer with a studio in Royal Oak, Michigan. Since 2008 he has expanded his business to include motorsports, product, and lifestyle photography.

Index